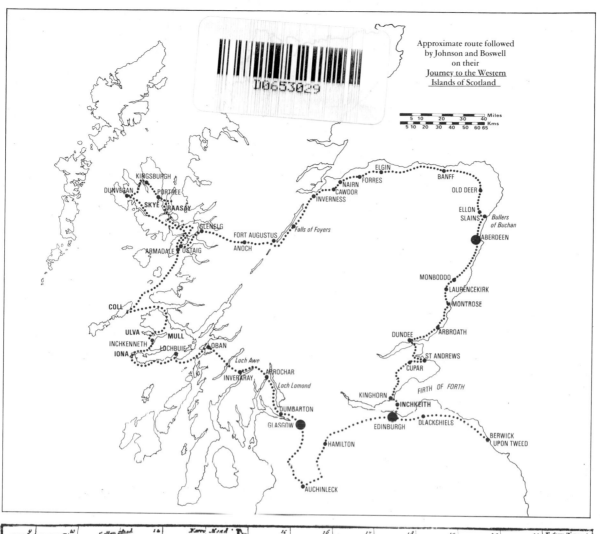

Approximate route followed
by Johnson and Boswell
on their
*Journey to the Western
Islands of Scotland*

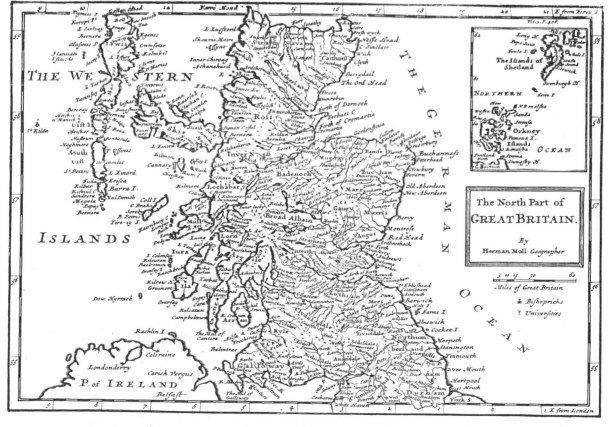

The North Part of
GREAT BRITAIN.

By
Herman Moll Geographer

A JOURNEY TO THE WESTERN ISLES

Johnson's Scottish Journey
Retraced by
Finlay J. Macdonald

A JOURNEY TO THE WESTERN ISLES

Johnson's Scottish Journey
Retraced by
Finlay J. Macdonald

MACDONALD & CO
LONDON & SYDNEY

All new text matter copyright
© Finlay J. Macdonald 1983

Original text first published 1785 as second edition
First published in Great Britain in
illustrated edition with introduction,
epilogue and other new text matter in 1983
by Macdonald & Co (Publishers) Ltd
    London & Sydney

Maxwell House
74 Worship Street
London EC2A 2EN

ISBN 0 356 09156 2

Printed and bound in Great Britain
by Hazell Watson & Viney Ltd, Aylesbury, Bucks

The author and publishers wish to thank the following for help in finding or permission to reproduce the black and white pictures on pages specified:

Angus District Museums, 25 and maps on 193; Arbroath Museum, 24 (photo © Macdonald 1983, by Jon Wyand); Oliver Brown, 126; the *Dundee Courier*, 19 (photo © D. C. Thomson and Co.); David Ellon Museum, 42; Glasgow Museum of Transport, 22; Macleod Photography, 46, 57; The Mansell Collection, 10, and period map on end-papers; the Mitchell Library, Glasgow, 21 and 27 (from *Antiquities of Scotland*), 49, 63, 87 – a Rowlandson print – and 91 r (from the Carruthers edition of Boswell's *Journal*), 31, 69, 90, 94, 156, 162 and 171 (Daniell prints), 38 and 181 (by Thomas Newte), 30 (lower, from *Old Landmarks of Aberdeen*), 32 and 55 (from *Remarkable*

Ruins of Great Britain), 26, 43, 183 and 187 (from *Scotland Sixty Years Ago*), 186 (a Sleezer print), and 18 and 23 (from *Theatrum Scotiae*); Calum Neish, 71, Graham Noble, 107; and Christine Ottewill, 188. The Scottish Tourist Board kindly provided the modern map of Scotland, adapted for use on end-papers. Illustrations on pages 14 (lower), 54, 65, 147 and 167 are taken from George Birbeck Hill's *Footsteps of Dr Johnson* (1800).

All colour, and the remaining black and white, photographs are by Jon Wyand and were specially commissioned by Macdonald & Co (Publishers) Ltd for this book.

Extracts from John Wain's *Samuel Johnson* appear by permission of Macmillan Publishers Ltd.

Contents

For Elizabeth Sutter who has helped me over parts of this journey as she has helped me in so many ways over the years.

Acknowledgements

'A man will turn over half a library to make one book,' and he will also turn the minds of half his literate friends.

All the libraries to which I had such frequent recourse treated me with the help and courtesy which I have come to expect from those institutions of cloistered sanity. I have frequented the Mitchell Library in Glasgow since I was a student in Glasgow University; it has renewed its youth while I have reneged mine, but it is even more than ever a house of light and learning through which I was ably guided by Fred Mitchell and John McGuire.

I owe thanks to people I have never met in person, like Mrs Gillian Zealand of the Arbroath Museum, and Miss Ann Matheson of the National Library of Scotland. Mr David Ellen of Nairn is only a voice on the telephone to me, but I am grateful for the resources of his Gallery. Donald MacCormick in Edinburgh is an old friend and I always come back from his Antiquarian Book Shop poorer in one sense and much richer in another.

In Inverness, Bill Sinclair will shortly get his bookshelves restored to their original capacity, and my brother Alex can answer his telephone in the knowledge that he isn't being ordered to explore some forgotten vennel in the Highland capital at dead of night. In Glasgow, Peter Pringle can return to his search for a place in the footlights none the worse for having rubbed shoulders with the author of *Irene*.

My own young son Finlay can return to the moving pictures on the television screen rather than counting still photographs on the dining room table!

Jon Wyand, whose photographer's eye has been such an inspiration, should really be expressing gratitude to me for having introduced him to the various ethnic attractions of the Highlands; and Bob Knowles and Richard Johnson of Macdonalds have gained a rich experience of Highland deadlines. The people who should be most grateful are the ones I've forgotten to mention because, for sure, nobody can attach blame to them.

Finlay J. Macdonald

Preface

THIS DOES NOT SET out to be a scholarly book but it is, I hope, a book that scholars may enjoy. Nor does it set out to be a Travel Guide, although I hope tourists and travellers to the Scottish Highlands may be tempted to take it with them for reference or, quite simply, for the passing of a wet evening should they, perchance, encounter a whiff of the kind of weather which beset the tenacious old traveller of two centuries ago. Not even the best efforts of the Scottish Tourist Board can guarantee Spanish sunshine in Skye in September, although it must be remembered that Dr Johnson was particularly unfortunate in the September that he chose! But today's visitor is, at least, guaranteed his creature comforts and he is highly unlikely to find a 'black Cyclops' jumping out of his bed, or have to share his bedroom with a minister who piddles in front of the maid!

There will be many who have never picked up the courage before to dip into the reputedly formidable prose of Dr Johnson, and many who have not yet summoned up the energy to venture north of the Highland Line. For them the series of brilliant colour photographs by Jon Wyand (in the strict sequence of the narrative but not firmly woven into it) provide a panorama of a Highland autumn such as I, as a Highlander myself, wish the old man had seen. The more I've lived with Johnson during the months of preparation of this book the more I've wished that there were more *sci-* and less *fi* in those epics of celluloid adventure in which past and present and future can be interchanged at the writer's whim, and that it were possible to knock on that door in Gough Square and say 'The Tardis is waiting, Doctor . . . let's have another look at the Highlands on the flip side of the centuries: you missed so much; so much that you didn't miss has changed; so much that you foresaw has happened.'

I encountered many difficulties in the preparation of this volume, and it would be idle to list them.

Suffice it to say that my greatest difficulty was, quite simply, that the more I worked with the Johnson text the more I found in it that I had missed before; the more I saw the twinkle in the eye behind a seemingly caustic comment of the kind that upset some early Scottish critics; the more I revelled in the ferocity of feeling behind some brief allusion to the corruption of the concepts of Chiefship in the eighteen century; the more I marvelled at the extrapolations of the philosophies of an oppressed society by a leading luminary from the society of the oppressors, and the more I understood that a great and receptive mind failed to appreciate a vernacular culture only because his interpreters were unable to bridge the culture gap for him. And, always, the more I progressed the more I wished I could go back to the beginning and start again.

All I have done, in fact, is attempt to present the 1785 Strahan and Cadell edition (usually regarded as the *second* edition) more or less as it was published, leaving in inconsistencies where they appeared to be Johnson's own inconsistencies or even oversights, and making only minor changes where I felt that eighteenth century gremlins were bedevilling the printer. Wherever possible I have tried to marry monochrome pictures (ancient and modern) to Johnson's narrative and my own commentary; in the case of the latter I confess that my own prejudices may not be a whit more forgiveable for being newer! Where some of Johnson's most interesting passages are long and discursive and philosophical it was felt wrong to force pictorial illustration for its own sake and, in the case of the colour photography in particular it has been left, as I have said, to stand as a running 'visual commentary' not on the text but on the tour itself — whose beauty must surely have escaped the half-blind, rain-soaked, ill-equipped man of words.

Finlay J. Macdonald

Winged Words

'I had desired to visit the Hebrides, or Western Islands of Scotland, so long, that I scarcely remember how the wish was originally excited; and was in the Autumn of the year 1773 induced to undertake the journey, by finding in Mr. Boswell a companion, whose acuteness would help my enquiry. . . .'

'Much may be made of a Scotchman, if he be caught young.'

'I know not any thing more pleasant, or more instructive, than to compare experience with expectation, or to register from time to time the difference between idea and reality.'

For a pleasant holiday — 'Turn all care out of your head as soon as you mount the chaise. Do not think about frugality; your health is worth more than it can cost. Do not continue any day's journey to fatigue. Take now and then a day's rest. Get a smart sea-sickness if you can. Cast away all anxiety, and keep your mind easy.'

Edinburgh Castle — 'It would make a good prison in England.'

To Boswell's wife who objected to their going to Skye on the grounds that it was 'bad country'. — 'Madam, we do not go there as to a paradise. We go to see something different from what we're accustomed to see.'

On his host in Skye, Sir Alexander Macdonald — 'It grieves me to see the chief of a great Clan appear to such disadvantage. This gentleman has talents, nay some learning; but he is totally unfit for this situation. Sir, the Highland Chiefs should not be allowed further south than Aberdeen. A strong minded man, like his brother Sir James, may be improved by an English education; but in general, they will be tamed into insignificance.'

Of his hostess, Lady Macdonald — 'This woman would sink a ninety gun ship; she is so dull, so heavy.'

On James Macpherson's 'Ossian' — 'Sir, a man might write such stuff forever, if he would *abandon* his mind to it.'

'If an epicure could remove by a wish, in quest of sensual gratifications, wherever he had supped he would breakfast in Scotland.'

'Sir, the noblest prospect which a Scotchman ever sees is the high road that leads him to England.'

'Seeing Scotland, Madam, is only seeing a worse England.'

Of Scotland — 'We must remember that He made it for Scotchmen; and comparisons are odious, but God made Hell.'

Of the Scots — 'Their learning is like bread in a besieged town; every man gets a little, but no man gets a full meal.'

'I have had my dinner exhilarated by the bagpipe, at Armidel, at Dunvegan, and in Col.'

'Those Highlanders that can speak English commonly speak it well, with few of the words, and little of the tone by which a Scotchman is distinguished.'

'Of the Earse language, as I understand nothing I cannot say more than I have been told. It is a rude speech of a barbarous people, who had few thoughts to express, and were content, as they conceived grossly, to be grossly understood.'

'Languages are the pedigree of a nation.'

Today Johnson's 'travelling garb' would probably attract no comment on the Inverness night train. Over a plain brown suit he wore a voluminous brown coat with capacious pockets. He arrived in Edinburgh armed with two pistols, but he was assured that he wouldn't need them north of Edinburgh and so he left them in the care of Boswell's wife. His walking-stick was a multi-purpose one; he found it a support for his weakened knees, and he had nails driven into it at 12" and 36" intervals so that he could use it as a measuring stick. It was his intention to present it to a museum at the end of his journey and he got very depressed when he lost it on Mull. He could see little hope of getting it back and cynically remarked to Boswell 'Consider the value of such a piece of timber here' — yet another jibe at the treelessness of Scotland.

Introduction

ON 6 AUGUST 1773 the greatest English literary figure of his day left his beloved London to embark on a journey which was to cover some 1,600 miles by post-chaise, horseback, and open boat through some wild territory and wintry seas. It was, in the words of a much later traveller, 'a brave, not to say desperate undertaking for an Englishmen of his customs and circumference'. He did not set out with the purpose of writing a book, and so the volume which ultimately appeared was one of retrospective impressions and philosophical extrapolations rather than a considered commentary on social conditions in the Scottish Highlands at the end of their most turbulent century. It is doubtful whether Dr Johnson could have produced an objective commentary. He was, after all, a high Tory and a committed Anglican venturing into a Scotland still reeling from Jacobitism and lurching into Presbyterianism. The book which he did write, however, has survived where countless successors have vanished or been consigned to obscure antiquarian archives; it has been reproduced in countless forms; it has tempted so many travellers to follow its route that if the Scottish Tourist Board were ever to elevate for itself a patron saint then he would surely be Samuel Johnson.

Johnson was born in Lichfield, the little cathedral town in Staffordshire, which also boasts of Joseph Addison and David Garrick. He was the son of Michael Johnson, an itinerant bookseller, and his wife Sarah who, like her Biblical namesake, embarked on motherhood at an advanced age. The son who was born to them, on Wednesday 18 September 1709, was hailed as 'a brave boy' by the male midwife who must have been a considerable optimist if he meant brave in the sense of 'fit' or 'sturdy', because by the end of his long life the newcomer was to fall victim to an awesome catalogue of infirmities, and acute hypochondria to make weight for those which he had escaped. In infancy he developed scrofula or tuberculosis of the Lymphatic System which was known then (and till very recently in the Scottish Highlands) as *King's Evil*; it was supposed to be curable only by a touch of the Royal hand, but Queen Anne was obviously not a successful practitioner and a visit to her failed to heal Johnson with the result that he went through life suffering from an increasing obesity which was the invariable evidence of the disease. Even if he had not inherited from his father a tendency to bouts of melancholy, his indifferent health would have been enough to induce it. He suffered from failing eyesight and defective hearing; the twitching limbs which Boswell found at times embarrassing was, probably, a form of St Vitus Dance; his admission about drink (that he could not 'take a *little* and therefore never touched it') almost certainly betokened an awareness of incipient alcoholism. It may be, after all, that George Hector, the male midwife, was not so far off the mark when he dubbed Michael Johnson's first born 'a brave boy'. It took more than a fair measure of bravery to survive such an affliction of ill-health and a journey to the Western Islands of Scotland forby!

Dr Johnson maintained that he had been eager to visit the Western Isles from boyhood; since his father had persuaded him to read what was probably the second earliest book of Hebridean travel – *A Description of the Western Islands of Scotland*, by Martin Martin. Martin – a native of Skye – made his tour of the Outer Hebrides in 1695 or thereabouts, and he included for good measure a brief account of life in the Orkney and Shetland islands as well. Martin was writing as an 'insider' and a Gaelic speaker and he captured (and was captivated by) the minutiae of Highland life of the period. While he purported to be concerned with the social and economic problems of the islands, and urged various Government actions for their improvement, he was forever being waylaid by the exotica – second sight, paganism, witchcraft and supernatural manifestations of all kinds. His book (first published in London in 1703) has run to several editions and is still a valuable social history of its period, but to the young and imaginative Samuel Johnson it must have read like an account of life on another planet even if he did in later life decry its literary merits and stated that 'No man now writes so ill as Martin's account of the Hebrides is written.' Mild criticism in comparison to some that his own efforts were to invite! But it may be that Martin inspired the dream of a feudal society existing within the British Isles – a dream which Johnson's journey was to destroy.

But if Martin Martin inspired such enthusiasm in the youthful genius from Lichfield why did he wait for the best part of half a century before succumbing to the curiosity which Martin had, allegedly, aroused? Was it indolence – from which he suffered in no small measure? Was it the disruption of the Jacobite Rising of 1745 which cut across his middle age and must have made Scotland appear an improbable place for a holiday jaunt? Or was it that success and fame had thirled him more closely to London and the intellectual society of which he was, himself, both the laureate and the éminence grise?

Certainly fame and fortune had come his way to the extent that he could throw Lord Chesterfield's gestures of patronage back in his face. From 1737 he had lived in London and, much as he hated writing, he had built up his formidable reputation on his contributions to *The Gentleman's Magazine* and, later, *The Rambler* which he himself founded; he had published his poem *London*, his *Life of Mr Richard Savage*, *The Vanity of Human Wishes*, and Garrick had produced his tragedy *Irene* which had proved profitable if barely prestigious. These, plus a plethora of other works, had been crowned by *A Dictionary of the English Language (1755)* which ran to five editions during his lifetime and put the seal on his fame as the eighteenth century's literary giant. It was that fame which, for two different reasons, made it inevitable that Samuel Johnson would visit Scotland and the Scottish Highlands whether he wanted to or not. First of all it brought into his life the man who was to be the sculptor of his immortality – James Boswell.

Boswell bounced, by anything but accident, into Johnson's life on 16 May 1763. The precise moment and location of the meeting were accidental, although Boswell had been trying to engineer an encounter for three years. When it took place in the back parlour of Thomas Davies's bookshop in Russell Street, Covent Garden, the 23-year-old Scot was overwhelmed but not, alas, tongue-tied. 'Mr Johnson,' he stumbled after Davies had maliciously revealed his nationality, 'I do indeed come from Scotland, but I cannot help it.' It was meant to be a pleasantry, teasing Johnson on his known bias

against Scotland and the Scots. Or so Boswell would have us believe. 'That,' replied Johnson 'is what a very great many of your countrymen cannot help.' There can have been few less propitious introductions to a friendship. But the friendship, between two men separated by nationality and attitudes and an age gap of thirty years, was to become one of the most fruitful associations of the world of literature.

From early on, Boswell was determined to coax *Mr* Johnson (as he was then) to visit Scotland, partly because – one would like to think – he genuinely wished to modify his guru's views on a country which the latter was to describe later as only 'a worse England'. There is no doubt that the idea had been initially planted by Johnson himself; he had casually mentioned Martin's book to Boswell within a couple of months of their first meeting and had gone so far as to hint by way of what Boswell took to be 'a very romantic fancy' that they might visit the Hebrides together after the younger man's return from his impending European tour, 'unless' Johnson had teased 'some very good companion had appeared in the interim'. No such good alternative companion would appear if Boswell could help it; the idea of showing off his new-found celebrated friend north of the border was one that appealed to Boswell's snobbish soul very much indeed. But the notion had to be left to simmer; in August 1763 Boswell set off on his European tour and did not return to London till February 1766. (It was during this period that Trinity College, Dublin, conferred on Johnson his Doctorate of Laws.)

Unbeknown to himself, and unrecognized as such, James Boswell had acquired an unexpected ally in his campaign to tempt Johnson to Scotland. In 1760, James Macpherson, a schoolmaster from Badenoch in the north of Scotland, had published *Fragments of Ancient Poetry collected in the Highlands of Scotland, and translated from the Gaelic or Erse language*. The publication had created a great deal of literary interest, but nothing compared with the excitement which greeted the appearance in 1762 of *Fingal, an ancient epic poem in six books*, and then, in 1763 (the year in which Boswell and Johnson met) *Temora*, another epic in eight books. Macpherson claimed them to be translations of Ossianic manuscripts which he had unearthed in various parts of the Highlands and Islands, and the poems were, allegedly, heroic verse dating back to the third century. They took Europe by storm. Goethe admired them. Napoleon carried a volume of them in his pocket. Johnson despised them and denounced them as fakes; when challenged as to whether he thought any man of a modern age could have written such poems he replied 'Yes, sir, many men, many women and many children.' He then went on to declare categorically that Macpherson's 'translations' were fakes. 'I believe there cannot be recovered, in the whole Erse language, five hundred lines of which there is any evidence to prove them a hundred years old. Yet I hear the father of Ossian boasts of two chests more of ancient poetry, which he suppresses, because they are too good for the English.'

His strictures on the quality of Macpherson's poetry were only half right. Had Macpherson admitted his poems to be (as they were) his own adaptations of fragments of original Gaelic poetry which he had, indeed, collected, he would have deserved some of the praise which the Romantic Age was so willing to confer on him. The tragedy for Macpherson was that he did not 'come clean' and continued to claim that he had manuscripts which he could not possibly produce. But, on the subject of Gaelic manuscripts, Johnson was wrong. *The Book of the Dean of Lismore*, for one, dates back to the very early sixteenth century. But, be that as it may, Johnson's vitriolic anger with Macpherson was, almost certainly, one further reason which tempted him north, to prove for himself that Gaelic or 'Erse' was incapable of producing literature such as Macpherson claimed for it.

By the Spring of 1773 Boswell was beginning to despair of bringing Johnson to commit himself to the journey, and so he changed his tactics. Through his father, the Scottish judge, Lord Auchinleck, Boswell had many influential contacts in Edinburgh, and he took to writing to them urging them to invite Dr Johnson north, in some cases pleading with them not to mention that they were being prompted to write. Most of them were only too

happy to oblige. The Chiefs of Clan Macdonald and Clan MacLeod pressed Johnson to visit their respective ancestral homes in Skye, and from Edinburgh and Aberdeen educational luminaries like Dr William Robertson and Professor James Beattie stressed the honour that a visit would confer on their cities. In London, Hester Thrale was keeping her promise to Boswell and using her wiles on Johnson. Whether or not the old man would have resisted those blandishments is now anybody's guess, but a powerful temptation had come his way in the form of Thomas Pennant's published accounts of *his* journeys through the Highlands in 1769 and 1772; they must have stirred memories of Martin Martin's book that he had read in his father's bookshop long ago.

Boswell had had to return home to Edinburgh in the early summer (he was by now a married man with a home in St James's Court) and it must have been with profound relief that he got a letter from Johnson finally committing himself to the Scottish tour.

August 3, 1773

Dear Sir, – I shall set out from London on Friday the 6th of this month, and purpose not to loiter much by the way

And on 6 August Dr Johnson finally left London sharing the cost of his post-chaise with Robert Chambers, Principal of New Inn Hall, Oxford, who was on a visit to his native Newcastle. Johnson loved the excitement of post-chaise travel but the cost of it was exorbitant. The one way trip to Edinburgh would have cost him about £22 and, apart from the pleasure of Chambers's company the chance of sharing the hire to Newcastle was not to be missed. On Tuesday 10 August he arrived in Newcastle and on the following Saturday he met Boswell in Boyd's Inn in Edinburgh. They were not to part company again for a hundred days.

Two centuries after Johnson this is how photographer Jon Wyand found White Horse Close.

On Saturday 14 August Dr Johnson arrived at last at the White Horse Inn at the head of White Horse Close. He had parted company with Principal Chambers at Newcastle and had shared the chaise for the rest of the journey with the lawyer William Scott who was later to be the judge of the High Court of Admiralty as Lord Stowell. In those days it was usual to call an inn by the name of its proprietor which is why Johnson's cryptic note to Boswell read 'Mr Johnson sends his compliments to Mr Boswell, being just arrived at Boyd's.' (Note he still called himself Mr Johnson although he had by then received his Doctorate from Trinity College, Dublin, and didn't hesitate to sign himself Dr in order to get medicine against prescription in Montrose!)

Edinburgh inns of the time were notoriously insalubrious — just as Edinburgh's sanitation was virtually non-existent — and by the time Boswell arrived at Boyd's Johnson had already tongue-lashed a waiter who had used his dirty fingers to put sugar into his lemonade. Nevertheless, by the time James Boyd, the proprietor of the White Horse Inn, retired he was worth

several thousand pounds which was a fortune even by hotel proprietor's standards nowadays.

By the time Lancelot Speed made this drawing (above) of White Horse Close for George Birbeck Hill in 1889 Boyd's Inn had already disappeared having served a presumably prosperous period as a brothel.

A Journey to the Western Islands of Scotland

I HAD DESIRED TO visit the *Hebrides*, or Western Islands of Scotland, so long, that I scarcely remember how the wish was originally excited; and was, in the Autumn of the year 1773, induced to take the journey, by finding in Mr. Boswell a companion whose acuteness would help my inquiry, and whose gaiety of conversation and civility of manners are sufficient to counteract the inconveniencies of travel in countries less hospitable than we have passed.

On the eighteenth of August we left Edinburgh, a city too well known to admit description, and directed our course northward, along the eastern coast of Scotland, accompanied the first day by another gentleman, who could stay with us only long enough to show us how much we lost at separation.

As we crossed the *Frith of Forth*, our curiosity was attracted by *Inch Keith*, a small island, which neither of my companions had ever visited, though, lying within their view, it had all their lives solicited their notice. Here, by climbing with some difficulty over shattered crags, we made the first experiment of unfrequented coasts. Inch Keith is nothing more than a rock covered with a thin layer of earth, not wholly bare of grass, and very fertile of thistles. A small herd of cows grazes annually upon it in the summer. It seems never to have afforded to man or beast a permanent habitation.

We found only the ruins of a small fort, not so injured by time, but that it might be easily restored to its former state. It seems never to have been intended as a place of strength, nor was built to endure a siege, but merely to afford cover to a few soldiers, who perhaps had the charge of a battery, or were stationed to give signals of approaching danger. There is, therefore, no provision of water within the walls, though the spring is so near, that it might have been easily enclosed. One of the stones had this inscription: "Maria Reg. 1564." It has probably been neglected from the time that the whole island had the same king.

We left this little island with our thoughts employed awhile on the different appearance that it would have made, if it had been placed at the same distance from London, with the same facility of approach; with what emulation of price a few rocky acres would have been purchased, and with what expensive industry they would have been cultivated and adorned.

When we landed, we found our chaise ready, and passed through *Kinghorn*, *Kirkaldy*, and *Cowpar*, places not unlike the small or straggling market-towns in those parts of England where commerce and manufactures have not yet produced opulence.

At Kinghorn the travellers dined at Monro's of fish with onion sauce, roast mutton and potatoes.

Johnson was delighted by the absence of tolls on the highways. He would have been less enthusiastic had he been taking his chaise across today's Tay Bridge.

Though we were yet in the most populous part of Scotland, and at so small a distance from the capital, we met few passengers.

The roads are neither rough nor dirty; and it affords a southern stranger a new kind of pleasure to travel so commodiously without the interruption of toll-gates. Where the bottom is rocky, as it seems commonly to be in Scotland, a smooth way is made indeed with great labour, but it never wants repairs; and in those parts where adventitious materials are necessary, the ground once consolidated is rarely broken; for the inland commerce is not great, nor are heavy commodities often transported otherwise than by water. The carriages in common use are small carts, drawn each by one little horse; and a man seems to derive some degree of dignity and importance from the reputation of possessing a two-horse cart.

ST. ANDREWS

At an hour somewhat late we came to St. Andrews, a city once archiepiscopal; where that university still subsists in which philosophy was formerly taught by Buchanan, whose name has so fair a claim to immortality as can be conferred by modern latinity, and perhaps a fairer than the instability of vernacular languages admits.

We found that, by the interposition of some invisible friend, lodgings had been provided for us at the house of one of the professors, whose easy civility quickly made us forget that we were strangers: and in the whole time of our stay we were gratified by every mode of kindness, and entertained with all the elegance of lettered hospitality.

In the morning we rose to perambulate a city which only history shews to have once flourished, and surveyed the ruins of ancient magnificence, of which even the ruins cannot long be visible, unless some care be taken to preserve them; and where is the pleasure of preserving such mournful memorials? They have been till very lately so much neglected that every man carried away the stones who fancied that he wanted them.

The cathedral, of which the foundations may be still traced, and a small part of the wall is standing, appears to have been a spacious and majestick building, not unsuitable to the primacy of the kingdom. Of the architecture, the poor remains can hardly exhibit, even to an artist, a sufficient specimen. It was demolished, as is well known, in the tumult and violence of Knox's reformation.

Not far from the cathedral, on the margin of the water, stands a fragment of the castle, in which the archbishop anciently resided. It was never very large and was built with more attention to security than pleasure. Cardinal Beatoun is said to have had workmen employed in improving its fortifications at the time when he was murdered by the ruffians of reformation, in the manner of which Knox has given what he himself calls a merry narrative.

During his stay in Edinburgh Dr Johnson had kept his High Anglican zeal in remarkable control and he had managed to view the humiliation of St Giles with commendable restraint, making only one caustic remark to Principal William Robertson — 'Come, let me see what was once a church.' But the desecration of St Andrews was too much for him. The whole of his commentary on his visit is clouded by his prejudice against Knox and the Reformers. Even the kindness of the professors did not contribute to abate the uneasy remembrance of a university declining, a college alienated, and a church profaned and hastening to the ground.

Two centuries have not confirmed Johnson's gloom. Today, St Andrews is one of the most attractive cities in Europe, with its development and restoration being carried through with immaculate concern for its historic past. The new University development on North Street is a splendid integration of new and old architecture, and the Crawford Centre for the Arts, which it houses, provides a marvellous milieu for the intermingling of town and gown and tourist. Far from declining, as Dr Johnson feared, St Andrews University (the oldest in Scotland) now has a student population carefully controlled to just over 3,000, with the greater proportion of them tending to come from outwith Scotland. The burgh itself has a population of only 12,000 with the result that, for most of the year, the visitor is very conscious of a University presence such as one tends to associate with Oxford or Cambridge.

In summer tourists take over, and St Andrews caters for a wide spectrum of visitors — from the sun-glassed hordes who crowd the North Sea beaches to the pebble-glassed scholastics who dodder through the carefully preserved ruins of the Cathedral and the Priory with more awe and less ire than did the old visitor of 1773. Equally lovingly preserved are the ruins of the old Castle (founded in 1200), and Dr Johnson might have been less perturbed by the dissolution of St Leonard's College had he foreseen that most of it would be resurrected and rebuilt as St Leonard's School for Girls.

Much of the credit for the continuing rehabilitation of Scotland's most atmospheric city must go to the St Andrews Preservation Trust whose motto might well be Johnson's own prophecy Where there is yet shame, there may in time be virtue.

Had Johnson and Boswell had more than two days in St Andrews the latter's eye — ever darting in search of the curious — would have been caught by the sight of a group of serious citizens lambasting a feather-stuffed ball round an open field with the kind of fanaticism nowadays associated with salmon fishers and ayatollahs. The Royal and Ancient Golf Club of St Andrews was already nineteen years old; today it is the mecca for hundreds of thousands of devotees from all over the world. The shade of Boswell may indeed haunt the exclusive bar of the Royal and Ancient Clubhouse today, but that of Johnson is more likely to frequent one of the many splendid coffee houses or the enterprising little Byre Theatre even although the latter has lost much of its quaintness in the course of modernization.

The change of religion in Scotland, eager and vehement as it was, raised an epidemical enthusiasm, compounded of sullen scrupulousness and warlike ferocity, which, in a people whom idleness resigned to their own thoughts, and who conversing only with each other, suffered no dilution of their zeal from the gradual influx of new opinions, was long transmitted in its full strength from the old to the young, but by trade and intercourse with England, is now visibly abating, and giving way too fast to that laxity of practice and indifference of opinion, in which men, not sufficiently instructed to find the middle point, too easily shelter themselves from rigour and constraint.

The city of St. Andrews, when it had lost its archiepiscopal pre-eminence, gradually decayed: One of its streets is now lost; and in those that remain there is the silence and solitude of inactive indigence and gloomy depopulation.

The university, within a few years, consisted of three colleges, but is now reduced to two: the college of St. Leonard being lately dissolved by the sale of its buildings and the appropriation of its revenues to the professors of the two others. The chapel of the alienated college is yet standing, a fabrick not inelegant of external structure; but I was always, by some civil excuse, hindered from entering it. A decent attempt, as I was since told, has been made to convert it into a kind of greenhouse, by planting its area with shrubs. This new method of gardening is unsuccessful; the plants do not hitherto prosper. To what use it will next be put I have no pleasure in conjecturing. It is something that its present state is at least not ostentatiously displayed. Where there is yet shame, there may in time be virtue.

The dissolution of St. Leonard's College was doubtless necessary; but of that necessity there is reason to complain. It is surely not

Dr Johnson would find the new University Library very spacious, but still 'elegant and luminous'. St Andrews University Library (refurbished and refitted within the last six years) is equipped with highly modern reference devices, and the staff are expert at dealing with researchers for books on Dr Johnson's visit to St Andrews!

without just reproach, that a nation, of which the commerce is hourly extending, and the wealth increasing, denies any participation of its prosperity to its literary societies; and, while its merchants or its nobles are raising palaces, suffers its universities to moulder into dust.

Of the two colleges yet standing, one is by the institution of its founder appropriated to Divinity. It is said to be capable of containing fifty students; but more than one must occupy a chamber. The library, which is of late erection, is not very spacious, but elegant and luminous.

The doctor, by whom it was shewn, hoped to irritate or subdue my English vanity, by telling me, that we had no such repository of books in England.

St. Andrews seems to be a place eminently adapted to study and education, being situated in a populous, yet a cheap country, and exposing the minds and the manners of young men neither to the levity and dissoluteness of a capital city, nor to the gross luxury of a town of commerce, places naturally unpropitious to learning: in one the desire of knowledge easily gives way to the love of pleasure, and in the other, is in danger of yielding to the love of money.

The students however are represented as at this time not exceeding a hundred. Perhaps it may be some obstruction to their increase that there is no episcopal chapel in the place. I saw no reason for imputing their paucity to the present professors; nor can the expense of an academical education be very reasonably objected. A student of the highest class may keep his annual session, or, as the English call it, his term, which lasts seven months, for about fifteen pounds, and one of lower rank for less than ten; in which board, lodging, and instruction are all included.

The Lord Rector is still the democratically elected representative of the students on the Court of the Scottish Universities. It used to be an honour conferred on eminent political or literary figures; now the selection can be occasionally eccentric or representative of popular tastes. This is Tim Brooke Taylor, co-writer and star of the zany television comedy series The Goodies being cheered through the streets of St Andrews after his election as Lord Rector in 1976.

The chief magistrate resident in the university, answering to our vice-chancellor, and to the *rector magnificus* on the continent, had commonly the title of Lord Rector; but being addressed only as *Mr. Rector* in an inauguratory speech by the present chancellor, he has fallen from his former dignity of style. Lordship was very liberally annexed by our ancestors to any station or character of dignity. They said the *Lord General* and *Lord Ambassador*; so we still say *my Lord* to the judge upon the circuit, and yet retain in our Liturgy *the Lords of the Council.*

In walking among the ruins of religious buildings we came to two vaults over which had formerly stood the house of the sub-prior. One of the vaults was inhabited by an old woman, who claimed the right of abode there, as the widow of a man whose ancestors had possessed the same gloomy mansion for no less than four generations. The right, however it began, was considered as established by legal prescription, and the old woman lives undisturbed. She thinks however that she has a claim to something more than sufferance; for as her husband's name was Bruce, she is allied to royalty, and told Mr. Boswell that when there were persons of quality in the place she was distinguished by some notice; that indeed she is now neglected, but she spins a thread, has the company of her cat, and is troublesome to nobody.

Having now seen whatever this ancient city offered to our curiosity, we left it with good wishes, having reason to be highly pleased with the attention that was paid to us. But whoever surveys

'Life has not many better things that this' Johnson once said of travelling by post-chaise. This is probably the type of two-horse chaise that he travelled in up the east coast of Scotland. A few years earlier he wouldn't have found one; the post-chaise had only reached as far north as Durham by 1758. The good state of the highways was thanks to an annual tax of six days' free labour extorted from poor people who couldn't afford to use them. The extortion is more subtle nowadays and, at least, it falls largely on the shoulders of the users!

the world must see many things that give him pain. The kindness of the professors did not contribute to abate the uneasy remembrance of a university declining, a college alienated, and a church profaned and hastening to the ground.

St. Andrews indeed has formerly suffered more atrocious ravages and more extensive destruction, but recent evils affect with greater force. We were reconciled to the sight of archiepiscopal ruins. The distance of a calamity from the present time seems to preclude the mind from contact or sympathy. Events long passed are barely known; they are not considered. We read with as little emotion the violence of Knox and his followers, as the irruptions of Alaric and the Goths. Had the university been destroyed two centuries ago, we should not have regretted it; but to see it pining in decay, and struggling for life fills the mind with mournful images and ineffectual wishes.

ABERBROTHICK

As we knew sorrow and wishes to be vain, it was now our business to mind our way. The roads of Scotland afford little diversion to the traveller, who seldom sees himself either encountered or overtaken, and who has nothing to contemplate but grounds that have no visible boundaries, or are separated by walls of loose stone. From the bank of the Tweed to St. Andrews I had never seen a single tree which I did not believe had grown up far within the present century. Now and then about a gentleman's house stands a small plantation, which in Scotch is called a *policy*, but of these there are few, and those few all very young. The variety of sun and shade is here utterly unknown. There is no tree for either shelter or timber. The oak and the thorn is equally a stranger, and the whole country is extended in uniform nakedness, except that in the road between *Kirkaldy* and *Cowpar* I passed for a few yards between two hedges. A tree might be a show in Scotland as a horse in Venice. At St. Andrews Mr. Boswell found only one, and recommended it to my notice; I told him it was rough, and low, or looked as if I thought so. This, said he, is nothing to another a few miles off. I was still less delighted to hear that another tree was not to be seen nearer. Nay, said a gentleman that stood by, I know but of this and that tree in the county.

The Lowlands of Scotland had once undoubtedly an equal portion of woods with other countries. Forests are everywhere gradually diminished, as architecture and cultivation prevail by the increase of people and the introduction of arts. But I believe few regions have been denuded like this, where many centuries must have passed in waste without the least thought of future supply. Davies observes in his account of Ireland, that no Irishman had ever planted an orchard. From that negligence some excuse might be drawn from an unsettled state of life, and the instability of property; but in Scotland possession has long been secure, and inheritance regular, yet it may be doubted whether before the Union any man between Edinburgh and England had ever set a tree.

Of this improvidence no other account can be given than that it probably began in times of tumult, and continued because it had begun. Established custom is not easily broken, till some great event shakes the whole system of things, and life seems to recommence upon new principles. That before the Union the Scots had little trade and little money is no valid apology; for plantation is the least expensive of all methods of improvement. To drop a seed into the ground can cost nothing, and the trouble is not great of protecting

The ruined Abbey of Arbroath is more than sacred in the Scottish tradition; it was here that The Declaration of Arbroath, *the definitive statement of Scotland's nationhood, was signed on 6 April 1320; it was to this place that the Stone of Destiny was returned after its temporary recovery from Westminster Abbey on Christmas Eve 1950.*

the young plant till it is out of danger; though it must be allowed to have some difficulty in places like these, where they have neither wood for palisades, nor thorns for hedges.

Our way was over the Firth of Tay, where, though the water was not wide, we paid four shillings for ferrying the chaise. In Scotland the necessaries of life are easily procured, but superfluities and elegancies are of the same price at least as in England, and therefore may be considered as much dearer.

We stopped a while at Dundee, where I remember nothing remarkable, and, mounting our chaise again, came about the close of the day to Aberbrothick.

The monastery of Aberbrothick is of great renown in the history of Scotland. Its ruins afford ample testimony of its ancient magnificence. Its extent might, I suppose, easily be found by following the walls among the grass and weeds, and its height is known by some parts yet standing. The arch of one of the gates is entire, and of another only so far dilapidated as to diversify the appearance. A square apartment of great loftiness is yet standing; its use I could not conjecture, as its elevation was very disproportionate to its area. Two corner towers particularly attracted our attention. Mr. Boswell, whose inquisitiveness is seconded by great activity, scrambled in at a high window, but found the stairs within broken, and could not reach the top. Of the other tower we were told that the inhabitants sometimes climbed it, but we did not immediately discern the entrance, and, as the night was gathering upon us, thought proper to desist. Men skilled in architecture might do what we did not attempt: They might probably form an exact ground-plot of this venerable edifice. They may, from some parts yet standing, conjecture its general form, and perhaps by comparing it with other buildings of the same kind and the same age, attain an idea very near to truth. I should scarcely have regretted my journey, had it afforded nothing more than the sight of Aberbrothick.

MONTROSE

Leaving these fragments of magnificence, we travelled on to Montrose, which we surveyed in the morning, and found it well built, airy, and clean. The town-house is a handsome fabrick with a portico. We then went to view the English chapel, and found a small church, clean to a degree unknown in any other part of Scotland, with commodious galleries, and, what was yet less expected, with an organ.

At our inn we did not find a reception such as we thought proportionate to the commerical opulence of the place; but Mr. Boswell desired me to observe that the innkeeper was an Englishman, and I then defended him as well as I could.

When I had proceeded thus far, I had opportunities of observing

This is one of the types of badges issued to the Montrose poor who were licensed to beg. Arbroath Museum has several examples of them.

*Painting of Montrose High Street,
showing the Town House.
(Unknown artist, 1826)*

what I had never heard, that there were many beggars in Scotland.
In Edinburgh the proportion is, I think, not less than in London,
and in the smaller places it is far greater than in English towns of
the same extent. It must, however, be allowed that they are not
importunate, nor clamorous. They solicit silently, or very modestly,
and therefore though their behaviour may strike with more force the
heart of a stranger, they are certainly in danger of missing the
attention of their countrymen. Novelty has always some power, an
unaccustomed mode of begging excites an unaccustomed degree of
pity. But the force of novelty is by its own nature soon at an end; the
efficacy of outcry and perseverance is permanent and certain.

The road from Montrose exhibited a continuation of the same
appearances. The country is still naked, the hedges are of stone, and
the fields generally plowed that it is hard to imagine where grass is
found for the horses that till them. The harvest, which was almost
ripe, appeared very plentiful.

Early in the afternoon Mr. Boswell observed that we were at no
great distance from the house of Lord Monboddo. The magnetism
of his conversation easily drew us out of our way, and the
entertainment which we received would have been a sufficient
recompense for a much greater deviation.

The roads beyond Edinburgh, as they are less frequented, must
be expected to grow gradually rougher; but they were hitherto by no
means incommodious. We travelled on with the gentle pace of a
Scotch driver who, having no rivals in expedition, neither gives
himself nor his horses unnecessary trouble. We did not affect the
impatience we did not feel, but were satisfied with the company of
each other as well riding in the chaise as sitting at an inn. The night

*The Bullers of Buchan. Still one
of the tourist attractions on the
road from Aberdeen to Peterhead.
The sea does indeed* boil *here,
and it was probably only
Johnson's myopia that allowed
him to take the crazy walk
around the rim.*

which in the spring chuse this place as convenient for incubation,
and have their eggs and their young taken in great abundance. One
of the birds that frequent this rock has, as we were told, its body not
larger than a duck's, and yet lays eggs as large as those of a goose.
This bird is by the inhabitants named a *Coot*. That which is called
Coot in England, is here a *Cooter*.

Upon these rocks there was nothing that could long detain
attention, and we soon turned our eyes to the *Buller*, or *Bouilloir* of
Buchan, which no man can see with indifference who has either sense
of danger or delight in rarity. It is a rock perpendicularly tubulated,
united on one side with a high shore, and on the other rising steep
to a great height, above the main sea. The top is open, from which
may be seen a dark gulf of water which flows into the cavity, through
a breach made in the lower part of the inclosing rock. It has the
appearance of a vast well bordered with a wall. The edge of the
Buller is not wide, and to those that walk round, appears very
narrow. He that ventures to look downwards sees that if his foot
should slip he must fall from his dreadful elevation upon stones on
one side or into the water on the other. We however went round,
and were glad when the circuit was completed.

When we came down to the sea, we saw some boats and rowers,
and resolved to explore the Buller, at the Bottom. We entered the
arch, which the water had made, and found ourselves in a place,
which though we could not think ourselves in danger, we could
scarcely survey without some recoil of the mind. The bason in which
we floated was nearly circular, perhaps thirty yards in diameter. We
were inclosed by a natural wall, rising steep on every side to a height
which produced the idea of insurmountable confinement. The
interception of all lateral light caused a dismal gloom. Round us

Inchkeith, in the middle of the Firth of Forth.

RIGHT
Inchkeith was strategically placed as a naval fortress. Between 1549 and 1567 it was garrisoned by the French for Mary of Guise.

OPPOSITE ABOVE
The students' library in the old part of St Andrews University.

OPPOSITE BELOW
Modern architecture in St Andrews University blends in harmoniously with the old.

BELOW
Kinghorn, now a quiet fishing village, was once the gateway to the hunting parks of the Scottish kings.

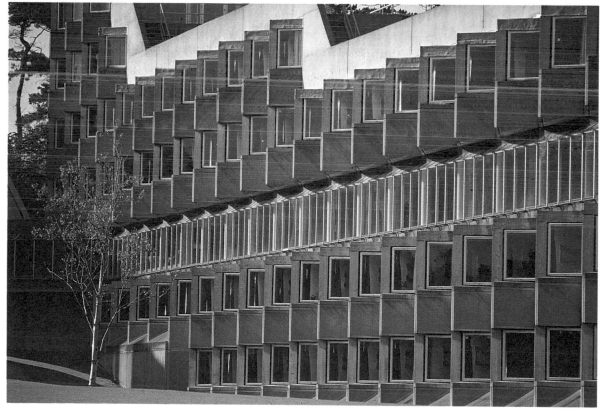

RIGHT
Dundee harbour. Its tranquillity belies the ravages of recession in this once great jute and shipping town.

OPPOSITE
Arbroath Abbey. Here the rays of Scottish nationalism fade when hope is highest and flicker when least expected.

BELOW
The Bishop's Palace, St Andrews.

44

RIGHT
King's College. The University of Old Aberdeen in the days when the city was divided in two. Now part of the city's great University.

BELOW
Old and new technologies meet in Aberdeen harbour.

LEFT
'This castle hath a pleasant seat . . .' The view from the site of MacBeth's Castle in Inverness across to the Black Isle. Birnham wood is well out of sight in the other direction!

BELOW
The south side of Loch Ness. The B 862 and B 852 approximately follow the old military road that Johnson travelled.

INVERNESS

Dun Macbeth, a charming Victorian villa, now stands on the reputed site of MacBeth's Castle, on Auldcastle Hill. The present Inverness Castle was built in the middle of the nineteenth century, on the site of two older castles. There is no trace of the fort which was occupied by Cromwell's soldiers when they were not teaching the Invernessians to make brogues and grow kail.

Abertarff House in Church Street is the oldest surviving house in Inverness, dating back to 1593. It was occupied at one time by the Frasers of Lovat. It was saved from ruin and restored by the National Trust for Scotland, and it is now the headquarters of An Comunn Gaidhealach, the principal body dedicated to the preservation and revival of the Gaelic language and culture.

Inverness was the last place which had a regular communication by high roads with the southern counties. All the ways beyond it have, I believe, been made by the soldiers of this century. At *Inverness*, therefore *Cromwell*, when he subdued *Scotland*, stationed a garrison, as at the boundary of the Highlands. The soldiers seem to have incorporated afterwards with the inhabitants, and to have peopled the place with an English race; for the language of this place has long been considered as peculiarly elegant.

Here is a castle, called the castle of Macbeth, the walls of which are yet standing. It was no very capacious edifice, but stands upon a rock so high and steep, that I think it was once not accessible, but by the help of ladders, or a bridge. Over against it, on another hill, was a fort built by *Cromwell*, now totally demolished; for no faction of Scotland loved the name *Cromwell*, or had any desire to continue his memory.

Yet what the Romans did to other nations, was in a great degree done by Cromwell to the Scots; he civilized them by conquest, and introduced by useful violence the arts of peace. I was told at *Aberdeen* that the people learned from Cromwell's soldiers to make shoes and to plant kail.

How they lived without kail, it is not easy to guess: They cultivate hardly any other plant for common tables, and when they had not kail they probably had nothing. The numbers that go barefoot are still sufficient to shew that shoes may be spared; they are not yet considered as necessaries of life; for tall boys, not otherwise meanly dressed, run without them in the streets; and in the islands, the sons of gentlemen pass several of their first years with naked feet.

I know not whether it be not peculiar to the Scots to have attained the liberal, without the manual arts, to have excelled in ornamental knowledge, and to have wanted not only the elegancies, but the conveniencies of common life. Literature soon after its renewal, found its way to *Scotland*, and from the middle of the sixteenth century, almost to the middle of the seventeenth, the politer studies were very diligently pursued. The Latin poetry of *Deliciae Poëtarum Scotorum* would have done honour to any nation, at least till the publication of *May's Supplement* the English had very little to oppose.

Yet men thus ingenious and inquisitive were content to live in total ignorance of the trades by which human wants are supplied, and to supply them by the grossest means. Till the Union made them acquainted with English manners, the culture of their lands was unskilful, and their domestick life unformed; their tables were coarse as the feasts of *Eskimeaux*, and their houses filthy as the cottages of Hottentots.

Since they have known that their condition was capable of improvement, their progress in useful knowledge has been rapid

and uniform. What remains to be done they will quickly do, and
then wonder, like me, why that which was so necessary and so easy
was so long delayed. But they must be for ever content to owe to the
English that elegance and culture, which, if they had been vigilant
and active, perhaps the English might have owed to them.

Here the appearance of life began to alter. I had seen a few women
with plaids at *Aberdeen*; but at *Inverness* the Highland manners are
common. There is, I think, a kirk in which only the Erse language
is used. There is likewise an English chapel, but meanly built,
where on Sunday we saw a very decent congregation.

We were now to bid farewell to the luxury of travelling, and to
enter a country upon which perhaps no wheel has ever rolled. We
could indeed have used our post-chaise one day longer, along the
military road to Fort *Augustus*, but we could have hired no horses
beyond Inverness, and we were not so sparing of ourselves, as to lead
them, merely that we might have one day longer the indulgence of
a carriage.

At Inverness, therefore, we procured, three horses for ourselves
and a servant, and one more for our baggage, which was no very
heavy load. We found in the course of our journey, the convenience
of having disencumbered ourselves, by laying aside whatever we
could spare; for it is not to be imagined without experience, how in
climbing crags, and treading bogs, and winding through narrow
and obstructed passages, a little bulk will hinder, and a little weight
will burden; or how often a man that has pleased himself at home

*The Old High Church and the
Free North Church. The former
was rebuilt in 1770, but
although the services were in
English it was Presbyterian and
Johnson wouldn't darken its
doors; the Free North Church
probably stands on the site of the
kirk in which only the Erse
language was used. The meanly
built chapel in which he found a
decent congregation has
disappeared long ago.*

Inverness. The Old High Church was rebuilt in 1770, *but the original spire is still retained.*

Shortly after leaving Inverness Johnson would have run out of roads anyway, so he decided to take the chafing 'road to the isles' on horseback. On two horses to be precise — although not at the same time. His weight made it necessary for him to switch ponies occasionally.

with his own resolution, will, in the hour of darkness and fatigue, be content to leave behind him everything but himself.

LOUGH NESS

We took two Highlanders to run beside us, partly to shew us the way, and partly to take back from the sea-side the horses, of which they were the owners. One of them was a man of great liveliness and activity, of whom his companion said, that he would tire any horse in Inverness. Both of them were civil and ready-handed. Civility seems part of the national character of Highlanders. Every chieftain is a monarch, and politeness, the natural product of royal government, is diffused from the laird through the whole clan. But they are not commonly dextrous: their narrowness of life confines them to a few operations, and they are accustomed to endure little wants more than to remove them.

We mounted our steeds on the thirteenth of August, and directed our guides to conduct us to Fort Augustus. It is built at the head of Loch Ness, of which *Inverness* stands at the outlet. The way between them has been cut by the soldiers, and the greater part of it runs along a rock, levelled with great labour and exactness, near the water-side.

Most of this day's journey was very pleasant. The day, though bright, was not hot; and the appearance of the country, if I had not seen the Peak, would have been wholly new. We went upon a surface so hard and level that we had little care to hold the bridle, and were therefore at full leisure for contemplation. On the left were high and steep rocks shaded with birch, the hardy native of the North, and covered with fern or heath. On the right the limpid waters of *Lough Ness* were beating their bank, and waving their surface by a gentle agitation. Beyond them were rocks sometimes covered with verdure, and sometimes towering in horrid nakedness. Now and then we espied a little corn field, which served to impress more strongly the general barrenness.

Lough Ness is about twenty-four miles long, and from one mile to two miles broad. It is remarkable that *Boethius* in his description of Scotland, gives it twelve miles of breadth. When historians or geographers exhibit false accounts of places far distant, they may be forgiven, because they can tell but what they are told; and that their accounts exceed the truth may be justly supposed, because most men exaggerate to others, if not to themselves: but *Boethius* lived at no great distance; if he never saw the lake, he must have been very incurious, and if he had seen it, his veracity yielded to very slight temptations.

Lough Ness, though not twelve miles broad, is a very remarkable diffusion of water without islands. It fills a large hollow between two ridges of high rocks, being supplied partly by the torrents which fall into it on either side, and partly, as is supposed, by springs at the bottom. Its water is remarkably clear and pleasant, and is imagined by the natives to be medicinal. We were told, that it is in some places a hundred and forty fathoms deep, a profundity scarcely credible, and which probably those that relate it have never sounded. Its fish are salmon, trout, and pike.

It was said at Fort *Augustus*, that *Lough Ness* is open in the hardest winters, though a lake not far from it is covered with ice. In discussing these exceptions from the course of nature, the first question is, whether the fact be justly stated. That which is strange is delightful, and a pleasing error is not willingly detected. Accuracy of narration is not very common, and there are few so rigidly philosophical, as not to represent as perpetual, what is only frequent, or as constant, what is really casual. If it be true that *Lough Ness* never freezes, it is either sheltered by its high banks from the cold blasts, and exposed only to those winds which have more power to agitate than congeal; or it is kept in perpetual motion by the rush of streams from the rocks that inclose it. Its profundity, though it should be such as is represented, can have little part in this exemption; for though deep wells are not frozen, because their water is secluded from the external air, yet where a wide surface is exposed to the full influence of a freezing atmosphere, I know not why the depth should keep it open. Natural philosophy is now one of the favourite studies of the Scottish nation, and *Lough Ness* well deserves to be diligently examined.

The road on which we travelled, and which was itself a source of entertainment, is made along the rock, in the direction of the lough; sometimes by breaking off protuberances, and sometimes by cutting the mass of stone to a considerable depth. The fragments are piled in a loose wall on either side, with apertures left at very short spaces, to give a passage to the wintry currents. Part of it is bordered with low trees, from which our guides gathered nuts, and would have had the appearance of an English lane, except that an English lane is almost always dirty. It has been made with great labour, but has this advantage, that it cannot, without equal labour, be broken up.

Within our sight there were goats feeding or playing. The mountains have red deer, but they came not within view; and if what is said of their vigilance and subtlety be true, they have some claim to that palm of wisdom which the eastern philosopher, whom Alexander interrogated, gave to those beasts which live furthest from men.

Near the way, by the water-side, we espied a cottage. This was the first Highland Hut that I had seen; and as our business was with life and manners, we were willing to visit it. To enter a habitation without leave, seems to be not considered here as rudeness or intrusion. The old laws of hospitality still give this licence to a stranger.

A hut is constructed with loose stones, ranged for the most part with some tendency to circularity. It must be placed where the wind cannot act upon it with violence, because it has no cement; and where the water will run easily away, because it has no floor but the naked ground. The wall, which is commonly about six feet high, declines from the perpendicular a little inward. Such rafters as can be procured are then raised for a roof, and covered with heath, which makes a strong and warm thatch, kept from flying off by ropes of twisted heath, of which the ends, reaching from the centre of the thatch to the top of the wall, are held firm by the weight of a large stone. No light is admitted but at the entrance, and through a hole in the thatch, which gives vent to the smoke. This hole is not directly over the fire, lest the rain should extinguish it; and the smoke therefore naturally fills the place before it escapes. Such is the general structure of the houses in which one of the nations of this opulent and powerful island has been hitherto content to live. Huts however are not more uniform than palaces; and this which we were inspecting was very far from one of the meanest, for it was divided into several apartments; and its inhabitants possessed such property as a pastoral poet might exalt into riches.

When we entered, we found an old woman boiling goats-flesh in a kettle. She spoke little English, but we had interpreters at hand; and she was willing enough to display her whole system of economy. She has five children, of which none are yet gone from her. The eldest, a boy of thirteen, and her husband, who is eighty years old,

Nowadays the devoted monster hunter can drive down the east side of Loch Ness. Johnson travelled along the army road constructed as part of the road network designed to subjugate the Highlands. Nobody appears to have told him about the monster although it had been seen by St Columba 1,200 years before, and is seen by somebody or other during most summers now. There is no certain trace now of the 'Highland Hut' which Boswell decided 'would be a scene for Mr Johnson'.

It was, indeed, Johnson's first glimpse of the interior of a black house (it would look rather like this reproduction of a Highland black house in Auchindrain Museum, Argyll) and his description of the Fraser house was to hold good for Highland black houses for a century and more. Johnson treated the old lady with his usual courtesy to ordinary people, but Boswell insisted on taking a lighted taper and viewing the poor woman's humble bedroom. It says much for her that she treated them with such hospitality; she would remember the day twenty-seven years earlier when another Englishman, one of the Duke of Cumberland's officers, had murdered her predecessor in that self-same house when she tried to stop him from raping her daughter. Had he but known it, Boswell's jokes about the old lady's fears that they wanted to go to bed with her were in poor taste.

(The front cover photograph is of the stone marking the site of the General's Hut where Johnson and Boswell spent the night.)

were at work in the wood. Her two next sons were gone to *Inverness* to buy *meal*, by which oatmeal is always meant. Meal she considered an expensive food, and told us, that in Spring when the goats gave milk, the children could live without it. She is mistress of sixty goats, and I saw many kids in an enclosure at the end of her house. She had also some poultry. By the lake we saw a potatoe-garden, and a small spot of ground on which stood four shucks, containing each twelve sheaves of barley. She has all this from the labour of their own hands, and for what is necessary to be bought, her kids and her chickens are sent to market.

With the true pastoral hospitality, she asked us to sit down and drink whisky. She is religious and though the kirk is four miles off, probably eight English miles, she goes thither every Sunday. We gave her a shilling, and she begged snuff; for snuff is the luxury of a Highland cottage.

Soon afterwards we came to the *General's Hut*, so called because it was the temporary abode of Wade while he superintended the works upon the road. It is now a house of entertainment for passengers, and we found it not ill stocked with provisions.

FALL OF FIERS

Towards evening we crossed by a bridge the river which makes the celebrated fall of Fiers. The country at the bridge strikes the imagination with all the gloom and grandeur of Siberian solitude. The way makes a flexure and the mountains, covered with trees, rise at once on the left hand and in the front. We desired our guides to shew us the fall, and dismounting clambered over very rugged craggs, till I began to wish that our curiosity might have been gratified with less trouble and danger. We came at last to a place where we could overlook the river, and saw a channel torn, as it seems, through black piles of stone, by which the stream is obstructed and broken, till it comes to a very steep descent, of such dreadful depth, that we were naturally inclined to turn aside our eyes.

But we visited the place at an unseasonable time, and found it divested of its dignity and terror. Nature never gives everything at once. A long continuance of dry weather, which made the rest of the way easy and delightful, deprived us of the pleasure expected from the fall of Fiers. The river having now no water but what the springs supply, showed us only a swift current, clear and shallow, fretting over the asperities of the rocky bottom, and we were left to exercise our thoughts, by endeavouring to conceive the effect of a thousand streams poured from the mountains into one channel, struggling for expansion in a narrow passage, exasperated by rocks rising in their way, and at last discharging all their violence of waters by a sudden fall through the horrid chasm.

The Falls of Foyers from Cordiner's Remarkable Ruins of Great Britain. *The famous falls were dry when Johnson visited them. Although he didn't know it then he was to discover to his cost that the long drought of 1773 was almost at an end! Today the falls are harnessed for an electricity dam, but their beauty has been retained.*

The way now grew less easy, descending by an uneven declivity, but without either dirt or danger. We did not arrive at Fort Augustus till it was late. Mr. *Boswell*, who, between his father's merit and his own, is sure of a reception wherever he comes, sent a servant before to beg admission and entertainment for that night. Mr. Trapaud, the governor, treated us with that courtesy which is so closely connected with the military character. He came out to meet us beyond the gates, and apologized that, at so late an hour, the rules of a garrison suffered him to give us entrance only at the postern.

FORT AUGUSTUS

In the morning we viewed the fort, which is much less than that of Ft. *George*, and is said to be commanded by the neighbouring hills. It was not long ago taken by the Highlanders. But its situation seems well chosen for pleasure, if not for strength; it stands at the head of the lake, and, by a sloop of sixty tuns, is supplied from Inverness with great convenience.

We were now to cross the Highlands towards the western coast, and to content ourselves with such accommodation as a way so little frequented could afford. The journey was not formidable, for it was but of two days, very unequally divided, because the only house, where we could be entertained, was not further off than a third of

the way. We soon came to a high hill, which we mounted by a military road, cut in traverses, so that as we went upon a higher stage, we saw the baggage following us below in a contrary direction. To make this way, the rock has been hewn to a level with labour that might have broken the perseverance of a Roman legion.

The country is totally denuded of its wood, but the stumps, both of oaks and firs, which are still found, shew that it has been once a forest of large timber. I do not remember that we saw any animals, but we were told that, in the mountains, there are stags, roebucks, goats, and rabbits.

We did not perceive that this tract was possessed by human beings, except that once we saw a corn field, in which a lady was walking with some gentlemen. Their house was certainly at no great distance, but so situated that we could not descry it.

Passing on through the dreariness of solitude, we found a party of soldiers from the fort, working on the road, under the superintendence of a serjeant. We told them how kindly we had been treated at the garrison, and as we were enjoying the benefit of their labours, begged leave to shew our gratitude by a small present.

Four of General Wade's roads intersect at Fort Augustus; the one taken by Johnson along Glen Moriston is now only a footpath. Fort Augustus is named after William Augustus, the infamous Duke of Cumberland. The military fort is now incorporated in part into tranquil Fort Augustus Abbey which is the successor to two old abbeys dating back to Columban days. The abbey now incorporates a famous boarding school for boys.

ANOCH

Early in the afternoon we came to Anoch, a village in Glenmollison,

This 'Wade' bridge in Glenmoriston is one of the forty or so bridges built by General Wade as part of his vast network of roads built for the pacification of the Highlands after the Jacobite Rising of 1715 – the pacification *which was intensified after the Forty Five and was still in process during Johnson's visit. Glenmoriston now has a magnificent hydro-electric dam – part of a more civilized network – near the cairn which marks the place where young Roderick Mackenzie was killed; he pretended to be Prince Charlie in order to give the latter a chance to escape hot pursuit; his head was presented to the Duke of Cumberland at Fort Augustus, thus gaining time and winning another narrow escape for the fugitive Prince.*

of three huts, one of which is distinguished by a chimney. Here we were to dine and lodge, and were conducted through the first room, that had the chimney, into another lighted by a small glass window. The landlord attended us with great civility, and told us what he could give us to eat and drink. I found some books on a shelf, among which were a volume or more of Prideaux's Connection.

This I mentioned as something unexpected, and perceived that I did not please him. I praised the propriety of his language, and was answered that I need not wonder, for he had learned it by grammar.

By subsequent opportunities of observation I found that my host's diction had nothing peculiar. Those Highlanders that can speak English, commonly speak it well, with few of the words and little of the tone by which a Scotchman is distinguished. Their language seems to have been learned in the army or the navy, or by some communication with those who could give them good examples of accent and pronunciation. By their Lowland neighbours they would not willingly be taught; for they have long considered them as a mean and degenerate race. These prejudices are wearing fast away; but so much of them still remains, that when I asked a very learned minister in the islands, which they considered as their most savage clans, *"Those,"* said he, *"that live next the Lowlands."*

As we came hither early in the day we had time sufficient to survey the place. The hut was built like other huts of loose stones,

Raining's School (recently demolished) was one of the two schools in Inverness. It was built in 1757 by a rich Norwich merchant and it attracted bright boys from all over the Highlands. The daughter of Johnson's host in Aonach almost certainly went to a similar school for girls which was also in Inverness on the site of Dunbar's Hospital, Church Street.

but the part in which we dined and slept was lined with turf and wattled with twigs, which kept the earth from falling. Near it was a garden of turnips and a field of potatoes. It stands in a glen, or valley, pleasantly watered by a winding river. But this country, however it may delight the gazer or amuse the naturalist, is of no great advantage to its owners. Our landlord told us of a gentleman, who possesses lands, eighteen Scotch miles in length, and three in breadth; a space containing at least a hundred square English miles. He has raised his rents to the danger of depopulating his farms, and he fells his timber, and by exerting every art of augmentation has obtained a yearly revenue of four hundred pounds, which for a hundred square miles is three half-pence an acre.

Some time after dinner we were surprised by the entrance of a young woman, not inelegant either in mien or dress, who asked us whether we would have tea. We found that she was the daughter of our host and desired her to make it. Her conversation, like her appearance, was pleasing. We knew that the girls of the Highlands are all gentlewomen, and treated her with great respect, which she received as customary and due, and was neither elated by it, nor confused, but repaid my civilities without embarrassment, and told me how much I honoured her country by coming to survey it.

She had been at *Inverness* to gain the common female qualifications, and had, like her father, the English pronunciation. I presented her with a book, which I happened to have about me, and should not be pleased to think that she forgets me.

In the evening, the soldiers whom we had passed on the road, came to spend at our inn the little money we had given them. They had the true military impatience of coin in their pockets, and had marched at least six miles to find the first place where liquor could be bought. Having never been before in a place so wild and unfrequented, I was glad of their arrival, because I knew that we had made them friends, and to gain still more of their good-will, we went to them, where they were carousing in the barn, and added something to our former gift. All that we gave was not much, but

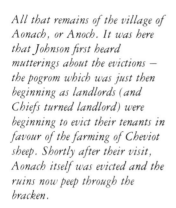

All that remains of the village of Aonach, or Anoch. It was here that Johnson first heard mutterings about the evictions — the pogrom which was just then beginning as landlords (and Chiefs turned landlord) were beginning to evict their tenants in favour of the farming of Cheviot sheep. Shortly after their visit, Aonach itself was evicted and the ruins now peep through the bracken.

it detained them in the barn, either merry or quarrelling, the whole night, and in the morning they went back to their work, with great indignation at the bad qualities of whisky.

We had gained so much the favour of our host, that, when we left his house in the morning, he walked by us a great way, and entertained us with conversation both on his own condition, and that of the country. His life seemed to be merely pastoral, except that he differed from some of the ancient Nomades in having a settled dwelling. His wealth consists of one hundred sheep, as many goats, twelve milk cows, and twenty-eight beeves ready for the drovers.

From him we first heard of the general dissatisfaction, which is now driving the Highlanders into the other hemisphere; and when I asked him whether they would stay at home if they were well treated, he answered with indignation, that no man willingly left his native country. Of the farm which he himself occupied, the rent had in twenty-five years been advanced from five to twenty pounds which he found himself so little able to pay, that he would be glad to try his fortune in some other place. Yet he owned the reasonableness of raising the Highland rents in a certain degree, and declared himself willing to pay ten pounds for the ground which he had formerly had for five.

Our host, having amused us for a time, resigned us to our guides. The journey of this day was long, not that the distance was great, but that the way was difficult. We were now in the bosom of the Highlands, with full leisure to contemplate the appearance and properties of mountainous regions, such as have been, in many countries, the last shelters of national distress, and are every where the scenes of adventures, stratagems, surprises, and escapes.

Mountainous countries are not passed but with difficulty, not merely from the labour of climbing; for to climb is not always necessary: but because that which is not mountain is commonly bog, through which the way must be picked with caution. Where there are hills, there is much rain, and the torrents pouring down the intermediate spaces seldom find so ready an outlet, as not to stagnate, till they have broken the texture of the ground.

Of the hills, which our journey offered to the view on either side, we did not take the height, nor did we see any that astonished us with their loftiness. Towards the summit of one, there was a white spot, which I should have called a naked rock, but the guides, who had better eyes, and were acquainted with the phaenomena of the country, declared it to be snow. It had already lasted to the end of August, and was likely to maintain its contest with the sun, till it should be reinforced by winter.

The height of mountains philosophically considered is properly computed from the surface of the next sea; but as it affects the eye or imagination of the passenger, as it makes either a spectacle or an obstruction, it must be reckoned from the place where the rise begins to make a considerable angle with the plain. In extensive continents the land may, by gradual elevation, attain great height without any other appearance than that of a plane gently inclined, and if a hill placed upon such raised ground be described, as having its altitude equal to the whole space above the sea, the representation will be fallacious.

These mountains may be properly enough measured from the inland base, for it is not much above the sea. As we advanced at evening towards the western coast, I did not observe the declivity to be greater than is necessary for the discharge of the inland waters.

We passed many rivers and rivulets, which commonly ran with a clear shallow stream over a hard pebbly bottom. These channels, which seem so much wider than the water that they convey would naturally require, are formed by the violence of wintry floods, produced by the accumulation of innumerable streams that fall in rainy weather from the hills, and bursting away with resistless impetuosity, make themselves a passage proportionate to their mass.

Such capricious and temporary waters cannot be expected to produce many fish. The rapidity of the wintry deluge sweeps them away, and the scantiness of the summer stream would hardly sustain them above the ground. This is the reason why in fording the northern rivers, no fishes are seen, as in England, wandering in the water.

Of the hills many may be called, with Homer's Ida, *abundant in springs*, but few can deserve the epithet which he bestows upon Pelion by *waving their leaves*. They exhibit very little variety; being almost wholly covered with dark heath, and even that seems to be checked in its growth. What is not heath is nakedness, a little diversified now and then by a stream rushing down the steep. An eye accustomed to flowery pastures and waving harvests is astonished and repelled by this wide extent of hopeless sterility. The appearance is that of matter incapable of form or usefulness, dismissed by nature from her care and disinherited of her favours, left in its original elemental state, or quickened only with one sullen power of useless vegetation.

It will very readily occur, that this uniformity of barrenness can afford very little amusement to the traveller; that it is easy to sit at home and conceive rocks and heath, and water-falls; and that these journeys are useless labours, which neither impregnate the imagination, nor enlarge the understanding. It is true that of far the greater part of things, we must content ourselves with such knowledge as description may exhibit, or analogy supply: but it is true likewise, that these ideas are always incomplete, and that at least, till we have compared them with realities, we do not know them to be just. As we see more, we become possessed of more certainties, and consequently gain more principles of reasoning, and found a wider basis of analogy.

Regions mountainous and wild, thinly inhabited, and little cultivated, make a great part of the earth, and he that has never seen them, must live unacquainted with much of the face of nature, and with one of the great scenes of human existence.

As the day advanced towards noon, we entered a narrow valley not very flowery, but sufficiently verdant. Our guides told us that the horses could not travel all day without rest or meat, and entreated us to stop here, because no grass would be found in any other place. The request was reasonable and the argument cogent. We therefore willingly dismounted and diverted ourselves as the place gave us opportunity.

I sat down on a bank, such as a writer of Romance might have delighted to feign. I had indeed no trees to whisper over my head, but a clear rivulet streamed at my feet. The day was calm, the air soft, and all was rudeness, silence, and solitude. Before me, and on either side, were high hills, which by hindering the eye from ranging, forced the mind to find entertainment for itself. Whether I spent the hour well I know not; for here I first conceived the thought of this narration.

We were in this place at ease and by choice, and had no evils to suffer or to fear; yet the imaginations excited by the view of an unknown and untravelled wilderness are not such as arise in the artificial solitude of parks and gardens, a flattering notion of self-sufficiency, a placid indulgence of voluntary delusions, a secure expansion of the fancy, or a cool concentration of the mental powers. The phantoms which haunt a desert are want, and misery, and danger; the evils of dereliction rush upon the thoughts; man is made unwillingly acquainted with his own weakness, and meditation shews

A stream in Glen Moriston. It was here, perhaps, that Dr Johnson sat down on a bank . . . and conceived the thought of this narration.

him only how little he can sustain, and how little he can perform. There were no traces of inhabitants, except perhaps a rude pile of clods called a summer hut, in which a herdsman had rested in the favourable seasons. Whoever had been in the place where I then sat, unprovided with provisions and ignorant of the country, might, at least before the roads were made, have wandered among the rocks, till he had perished with hardship, before he could have found either food or shelter. Yet what are these hillocks to the ridges of Taurus, or these spots of wildness to the desarts of America?

It was not long before we were invited to mount, and continued our journey along the side of a lough, kept full by many streams, which with more or less rapidity and noise crossed the road from the hills on the other hand. These currents, in their diminished state, after several dry months, afford, to one who has always lived in level countries, an unusual and delightful spectacle; but in the rainy season, such as every winter may be expected to bring, must precipitate an impetuous and tremendous flood. I suppose the way by which we went, is at that time impassable.

GLENSHEALS

The lough at last ended in a river broad and shallow like the rest, but that it may be passed when it is deeper there is a bridge over it. Beyond it is a valley called *Glensheals*, inhabited by the clan Macrae. Here we found a village called *Auknasheals*, consisting of many huts, perhaps twenty, built all of *dry-stone*, that is, stones piled up without mortar.

We had, by the direction of the officers at Fort *Augustus*, taken bread for ourselves, and tobacco for those Highlanders who might

The valley of Glenshiel, scene of the Battle of Glenshiel (1719). One of the lesser known abortive Jacobite Risings in which the Macraes and the Mackenzies under the Earl of Seaforth were heavily defeated by Hanoverian troops. The Glen was still being patrolled from the Bernera Barracks by soldiers such as Johnson and Boswell entertained.

show us any kindness. We were now at a place where we could obtain milk, but must have wanted bread if we had not brought it. The people of this valley did not appear to know any English, and our guides now became doubly necessary as interpreters. A woman, whose hut was distinguished by greater spaciousness and better architecture, brought out some pails of milk. The villagers gathered about us in considerable numbers, I believe without any evil intention, but with a very savage wildness of aspect and manner. When our meal was over, Mr. *Boswell* sliced the bread, and divided it amongst them, as he supposed them never to have tasted a wheaten loaf before. He then gave them little pieces of twisted tobacco, and among the children we distributed a small handful of halfpence, which they received with great eagerness. Yet I have been since told, that the people of that valley are not indigent; and when we mentioned them afterwards as needy and pitiable, a Highland lady let us know that we might spare our commiseration; for the dame whose milk we drank had probably more than a dozen milk cows. She seemed unwilling to take any price, but being pressed to make a demand, at last named a shilling. Honesty is not greater where elegance is less. One of the by-standers, as we were told afterwards, advised her to ask more, but she said a shilling was enough. We gave her half-a-crown, and I hope got some credit by our behaviour; for the company said, if our interpreters did not flatter us, that they had not seen such a day since the old laird of Macleod passed through the country.

Johnson dispensing largesse to Highland children. From Carruthers's edition of Boswell's Journal.

The Macraes, as we heard afterwards in the Hebrides, were originally an indigent and subordinate clan, and having no farms nor stock, were in great numbers servants to the Maclellans who, in the wars of Charles the First, took arms at the call of the heroic *Montrose*, and were, in one of his battles, almost all destroyed. The women that were left at home, being thus deprived of their husbands, like the Scythian ladies of old, married their servants, and the Macraes became a considerable race.

THE HIGHLANDS

As we continued our journey, we were at leisure to extend our speculations, and to investigate the reason of those peculiarities by which such rugged regions as those before us are generally distinguished.

Mountainous countries commonly contain the original, at least the oldest race of inhabitants, for they are not easily conquered, because they must be entered by narrow ways, exposed to every power of mischief from those that occupy the heights; and every new ridge is a new fortress where the defendants have again the same advantages. If the assailants either force the strait, or storm the summit, they gain only so much ground; their enemies are fled to take possession of the next rock, and the pursuers stand at gaze, knowing neither where the ways of escape wind among the steeps, nor where the bog has firmness to sustain them: besides that, mountaineers have an agility in climbing and descending distinct from strength and courage, and attainable only by use.

If the war be not soon concluded, the invaders are dislodged by hunger; for in those anxious and toilsome marches provisions cannot easily be carried, and are never to be found. The wealth of mountains is cattle which, while the men stand in the passes, the women drive away. Such lands at last cannot repay the expence of conquest, and therefore perhaps have not been so often invaded by the mere ambition of dominion; as by resentment of robberies and insults, or the desire of enjoying in security the more fruitful provinces.

As mountains are long before they are conquered, they are likewise long before they are civilised. Men are softened by intercourse mutually profitable, and instructed by comparing their own notions with those of others. Thus Caesar found the maritime parts of Britain made less barbarous by their commerce with the Gauls. Into a barren and rough tract no stranger is brought either by the hope of gain or of pleasure. The inhabitants having neither commodities for sale, nor money for purchase, seldom visit more polished places, or if they do visit them seldom return.

It sometimes happens that by conquest, intermixture, or gradual refinement, the cultivated parts of a country change their language. The mountaineers then become a distinct nation, cut off by dissimilitude of speech from conversation with their neighbours. Thus in Biscay, the original Cantabrian, and in Dalecarlia, the old Swedish still subsists. Thus Wales and the Highlands speak the tongue of the first inhabitants of Britain, while the other parts have received first the Saxon, and in some degree afterwards the French, and then formed a third language between them.

That the primitive manners are continued where the primitive language is spoken, no nation will desire me to suppose, for the manners of mountaineers are commonly savage, but they are rather produced by their station than derived from their ancestors.

Such seems to be the disposition of man, that whatever makes a distinction produces rivalry. England, before other causes of enmity were found, was disturbed for some centuries by the contests of the northern and southern counties; so that at Oxford, the peace of study could for a long time be preserved only by chusing annually one of the proctors from each side of the Trent. A tract intersected by many ridges of mountains, naturally divides its inhabitants into petty nations, which are made by a thousand causes enemies to each other. Each will exalt its own chiefs, each will boast the valour of its men, or the beauty of its women; and every claim of superiority irritates competition; injuries will sometimes be done, and be more injuriously defended; retaliation will sometimes be attempted, and the debt exacted with too much interest.

In the Highlands it was a law, that if a robber was sheltered from justice, any man of the same clan might be taken in his place. This

Bernera Barracks, built after the Battle of Glenshiel. From here, the army policed effectively for many years from Glenelg to Glenmoriston.

was a kind of irregular justice, which, though necessary in savage times, could hardly fail to end in a feud, and a feud once kindled among an idle people with no variety of pursuits to divert their thoughts, burnt on for ages either sullenly glowing in secret mischief, or openly blazing into public violence. Of the effects of this violent judicature there are not wanting memorials. The cave is now to be seen to which one of the Campbells, who had injured the Macdonalds, retired with a body of his own clan. The Macdonalds required the offender, and being refused, made a fire at the mouth of the cave, by which he and his adherents were suffocated together.

Mountaineers are warlike, because by their feuds and competitions they consider themselves as surrounded with enemies, and are always prepared to repel incursions, or to make them. Like the Greeks in their unpolished state, described by Thucydides, the Highlanders, till lately, went always armed, and carried their weapons to visits and to church.

Mountaineers are thievish, because they are poor, and, having neither manufactures nor commerce, can grow richer only by robbery. They regularly plunder their neighbours, for their neighbours are commonly their enemies; and having lost that reverence for property, by which the order of civil life is preserved, soon consider all as enemies, whom they do not reckon as friends, and think themselves licensed to invade whatever they are not obliged to protect.

By a strict administration of the laws, since the laws have been introduced into the Highlands, this disposition to thievery is very much repressed. Thirty years ago no herd had ever been conducted through the mountains without paying tribute in the night to some of the clans; but cattle are now driven, and passengers travel without danger, fear, or molestation.

Among a warlike people, the quality of highest esteem is personal courage, and with the ostentatious display of courage are closely connected promptitude of offence and quickness of resentment. The Highlanders, before they were disarmed, were so addicted to quarrels, that the boys used to follow any publick procession or ceremony, however festive, or however solemn, in expectation of the battle, which was sure to happen before the company dispersed.

Mountainous regions are sometimes so remote from the seat of government, and so difficult to access, that they are very little under the influence of the sovereign, or within the reach of national justice. Law is nothing without power; and the sentence of a distant court could not be easily executed, nor perhaps very safely promulgated, among men ignorantly proud and habitually violent, unconnected with the general system, and accustomed to reverence only their own lords. It has therefore been necessary to erect many particular jurisdictions, and commit the punishment of crimes, and the decision of right to the proprietors of the country who could enforce their own decrees. It immediately appears that such judges will be often ignorant, and often partial; but in the immaturity of political establishments no better expedient could be found. As government advances towards perfection, provincial judicature is perhaps in every empire gradually abolished.

Those who had thus the dispensation of law, were by conscience themselves lawless. Their vassals had no shelter from outrages and oppressions; but were condemned to endure, without resistance, the caprices of wantonness, and the rage of cruelty.

In the Highlands, some great lords had a hereditary jurisdiction over counties, and some chieftains over their own lands; till the final conquest of the Highlands afforded an opportunity of crushing all the local courts, and of extending the general benefits of equal law to the low and the high, in the deepest recesses and obscurest corners.

While the chiefs had this resemblance of royalty, they had little inclination to appeal, on any question, to superior judicatures. A claim of lands between two powerful lairds was decided like a contest for dominion between sovereign powers. They drew their forces into the field, and right attended on the strongest. This was, in ruder times, the common practice, which the kings of Scotland could seldom control.

Even so lately as in the last years of King William, a battle was fought at *Mull Roy*, on a plain a few miles to the south of Inverness, between the clans of *Mackintosh* and *Macdonald* of *Keppoch*. *Col. Macdonald*, the head of a small clan, refused to pay the dues demanded from him by *Mackintosh*, as his superior lord. They disdained the interposition of judges and laws, and calling each his followers to maintain the dignity of the clan, fought a formal battle, in which several considerable men fell on the side of *Mackintosh*,

without a complete victory to either. This is said to have been the last open war made between clans by their own authority.

The Highland lords made treaties, and formed alliances, of which some traces may still be found, and some consequences still remain as lasting evidences of petty regality. The terms of one of these confederacies were, that each should support the other in the right, or in the wrong, except against the king.

The inhabitants of mountains form distinct races, and are careful to preserve their genealogies. Men in a small district necessarily mingle blood by intermarriages, and combine at last into one family, with a common interest in the honour and disgrace of every individual. Then begins that union of affections, and co-operation of endeavours, that constitute a clan. They who consider themselves as ennobled by their family, will think highly of their progenitors, and they who through successive generations live always together in the same place, will preserve local stories and hereditary prejudices. Thus every Highlander can talk of his ancestors, and recount the outrages which they suffered from the wicked inhabitants of the next valley.

Such are the effects of habitation among mountains, and such were the qualities of the Highlanders, while their rocks secluded them from the rest of mankind, and kept them an unaltered and discriminated race. They are now losing their distinction, and hastening to mingle with the general community.

The passenger ferry, Glenelg. To reach Glenelg the travellers had to negotiate the steep and dangerous Pass of Mam Ratagan (1,100 feet). This was one of the occasions when Johnson had to be prevailed upon to keep switching horses because of his weight. Although he doesn't dwell on his hardships he was tired and more than a little frightened, but he was able to joke 'Goodbye Mam Ratagan, I hope I never see your face again.'

GLENELG

We left *Auknasheals* and the *Macraes* in the afternoon, and in the evening came to *Ratiken*, a high hill on which a road is cut, but so steep and narrow that it is very difficult. There is now a design of making another way round the bottom. Upon one of the precipices, my horse, weary with the steepness of the rise, staggered a little, and I called in haste to the Highlander to hold him. This was the only moment of my journey, in which I thought myself endangered.

Having surmounted the hill at last, we were told that at *Glenelg*, on the sea-side, we should come to a house of lime and slate and glass. This image of magnificence raised our expectation. At last we came to our inn weary and peevish, and began to inquire for meat and beds.

Of the provisions the negative catalogue was very copious. Here was no meat, no milk, no bread, no eggs, no wine. We did not express much satisfaction. Here, however, we were to stay. Whisky we might have, and I believe at last they caught a fowl and killed it. We had some bread, and with that we prepared ourselves to be contented, when we had a very eminent proof of Highland hospitality. Along some miles of the way, in the evening, a gentleman's servant had kept us company on foot with very little notice on our part. He left us near *Glenelg*, and we thought on him no more till he came to us again, in about two hours, with a present from his master of rum and sugar. The man had mentioned his company, and the gentleman, whose name, I think, is *Gordon*, well knowing the penury of the place, had this attention to two men, whose names perhaps he had not heard, by whom his kindness was not likely to be ever repaid, and who could be recommended to him only by their necessities.

We were now to examine our lodging. Out of one of the beds on which we were to repose, started up, at our entrance, a man black as a Cyclops from the forge. Other circumstances of no elegant recital concurred to disgust us. We had been frighted by a lady at Edinburgh, with discouraging representations of Highland lodgings. Sleep, however, was necessary. Our Highlanders had at last found some hay, with which the inn could not supply them. I directed them to bring a bundle into the room, and slept upon it in my riding coat. Mr. Boswell, being more delicate, laid himself sheets with hay over and under him, and lay in linen like a gentleman.

SKY. ARMYDEL

In the morning, September the twentieth, we found ourselves on the edge of the sea. Having procured a boat, we dismissed our Highlanders, whom I would recommend to the service of any future travellers, and were ferried over to the isle of Sky. We landed at *Armidel*, where we were met on the sands by Sir Alexander

Macdonald, who was at that time there with his lady, preparing to leave the island and reside at Edinburgh.

Armidel is a neat house, built where the *Macdonalds* had once a seat, which was burnt in the commotions that followed the Revolution. The walled orchard, which belonged to the former house, still remains. It is well shaded by tall ash trees, of a species, as Mr. Janes the fossilist informed me, uncommonly valuable. This plantation is very properly mentioned by Dr. *Campbell* in his new account of the state of *Britain*, and deserves attention; because it proves that the present nakedness of the *Hebrides* is not wholly the fault of nature.

As we sat at Sir Alexander's table, we were entertained, according to the ancient usage of the north, with the melody of the bagpipe. Everything in those countries has its history. As the bagpiper was playing, an elderly gentleman informed us, that in some remote time, the *Macdonalds* of Glengary having been injured, or offended by the inhabitants of *Culloden*, and resolving to have justice or vengeance, came to *Culloden* on a Sunday, where finding their enemies at worship, they shut them all up in the church, which they set on fire; and this, said he, is the tune that the piper played while they were burning.

Narrations like this, however uncertain, deserve the notice of a traveller, because they are the only records of a nation that has no historians, and afford the most genuine representation of the life and character of the ancient Highlanders.

Under the domination of *Highlander* are comprehended in Scotland

Armadale — seat of Clan Donald from the time that they vacated Duntulm in the north of Skye in 1732. William Daniell, the artist of this aquatint, was embellishing on the draft plans for the castle which was not, in fact, completed in the year of publication — 1813. Johnson and Boswell spent their unhappy days in Armadale in the house of Sir Alexander Macdonald's factor, which Sir Alexander used during his visits to Skye.

all that now speak the Erse language, or retain the primitive manners, whether they live among the mountains or in the islands; and in that sense I use the name when there is not some apparent reason for making a distinction.

In *Sky* I first observed the use of Brogues, a kind of artless shoes, stitched with thongs so loosely, that though they defend the foot from stones, they do not exclude water. Brogues were formerly made of raw hides, with their hair inwards, and such are perhaps still used in rude and remote parts; but they are said not to last above two days. Where life is somewhat improved, they are now made of leather tanned with oak bark, as in other places, or with the bark of birch, or roots of tormentil, a substance recommended in defect of bark, about forty years ago, to the Irish tanners, by one to whom the parliament of that kingdom voted a reward. The leather of *Sky* is not completely penetrated by vegetable matter, and therefore cannot be very durable.

My inquiries about brogues, gave me an early specimen of Highland information. One day I was told, that to make brogues was a domestick art, which every man practised for himself, and that a pair of brogues was the work of one hour. I supposed that the husband made brogues as the wife made an apron, till next day it was told me, that a brogue-maker was a trade, and that a pair would cost half-a-crown. It will easily occur that these representations may both be true, and that, in some places, man may buy them, and in others, make them for themselves; but I had both the accounts in the same house within two days.

Many of my subsequent inquiries upon more interesting topicks ended in the like uncertainty. He that travels in the Highlands may easily saturate his soul with intelligence, if he will acquiesce in the first account. The Highlander gives to every question an answer so prompt and peremptory, that scepticism itself is dared into silence, and the mind sinks before the bold reporter in unresisting credulity; but if a second question be ventured, it breaks the enchantment; for it is immediately discovered that what was told so confidently was told at a hazard, and that such fearlessness of assertion was either the sport of negligence or the refuge of ignorance.

If individuals are thus at variance with themselves, it can be no wonder that the accounts of different men are contradictory. The traditions of an ignorant and savage people have been for ages negligently heard, and unskilfully related. Distant events must have been mingled together, and the actions of one man given to another. These, however, are deficiencies in story, for which no man is now to be censured. It were enough, if what there is yet opportunity of examining were accurately inspected, and justly represented; but such is the laxity of Highland conversation, that the inquirer is kept in continual suspense, and by a kind of intellectual retrogradation, knows less as he hears more.

Clan Donald were once the most powerful and numerous of the Highland Clans. At the height of their power they formed the Lordship of the Isles (1354– 1493) and held sway over territories extending from Lewis down to the Isle of Man, and on mainland Scotland as far east as Inverness. The Lordship was a highly sophisticated organization with its own medical and legal systems, and it represented the Clan system at its very best. It became so powerful that it became a threat to the Scottish monarchy and it was dissolved by King James IV in 1493 with the king's eldest son assuming the title of 'Lord of the Isles' in perpetuity. (The present Lord of the Isles is Prince Charles.)

After the dissolution of the Lordship the different branches of Clan Donald (Macdonald of Clanranald, Macdonald of Keppoch etc.) were allowed to retain their individual chiefships with Macdonald of Sleat (one of whom was Johnson's host) being accepted as High Chief. After the Forty Five, and during the traumatic years of exploitation for the kelp industry, eviction and famine,

the record of the Macdonalds of Sleat was deplorable and Johnson was more than kind in his denunciation of Sir Alexander's attitudes.

Johnson's host became the first Lord Macdonald (an Irish peerage) in 1795.

After a period of ill-gained wealth and prosperity the Chiefs of Sleat fell on less fortunate days, and the present Lord, Godfrey Macdonald, inherited a depleted estate and a mountain of death duties. Most of the remainder of the old estates of Sleat were sold off; some of the lands around Armadale Castle and the remains of the castle itself were acquired by the Clan Donald Lands Trust (spearheaded by wealthy clan members in America) and a Clan Centre was established in the grounds of the old castle in 1976.

The present Lord Macdonald (fifth from the left) is seen here flanked by the chiefs of various branches of Clan Donald and members of the Clan Donald Lands Trust.

In the islands the plaid is rarely worn. The law by which the Highlanders have been obliged to change the form of their dress, has, in all the places that we have visited, been universally obeyed. I have seen only one gentleman completely clothed in the ancient habit, and by him it was worn only occasionally and wantonly. The common people do not think themselves under any legal necessity of having coats; for they say that the law against plaids was made by Lord Hardwicke, and was in force only for his life; but the same poverty that made it then difficult for them to change their clothing, hinders them now from changing it again.

The filibeg, or lower garment, is still very common, and the bonnet almost universal; but their attire is such as produces, in a sufficient degree, the effect intended by the law, of abolishing the dissimilitude of appearance between the Highlanders and the other inhabitants of Britain; and if dress be supposed to have much influence, facilitates their coalition with their fellow-subjects.

What we have long used we naturally like, and therefore the Highlanders were unwilling to lay aside their plaid, which yet to an unprejudiced spectator must appear an incommodious and cumbersome dress; for hanging loosely upon the body, it must flutter in a quick motion, or require one of the hands to keep it close. The Romans always laid aside the gown when they had anything to do. It was a dress so unsuitable to war, that the same word which signified a gown signified peace. The chief use of a plaid seems to be this, that they could commodiously wrap themselves in it, when they were obliged to sleep without a better cover.

In our passage from *Scotland* to *Sky*, we were wet for the first time with a shower. This was the beginning of the Highland winter, after which we were told that a succession of three dry days was not to be expected for many months. The winter of the *Hebrides* consists of little more than rain and wind. As they are surrounded by an ocean never frozen, the blasts that come to them over the water are too much softened to have the power of congelation. The salt loughs, or inlets of the sea, which shoot very far into the island, never have any ice upon them, and the pools of fresh water will never bear the walker. The snow that sometimes falls, is soon dissolved by the air, or the rain.

This is not the description of a cruel climate, yet the dark months are here a time of great distress; because the summer can do little more than feed itself, and winter comes with its cold and its scarcity upon families very slenderly provided.

CORIATACHAN IN SKY

The third or fourth day after our arrival at *Armidel* brought us an invitation to the isle of *Raasay*, which lies east of *Sky*. It is incredible how soon the account of any event is propagated in these narrow

countries by the love of talk, which much leisure produces, and the relief given to the mind in the penury of insular conversation by a new topick. The arrival of strangers at a place so rarely visited excites rumour, and quickens curiosity. I know not whether we touched at any corner where Fame had not already prepared us a reception.

To gain a commodious passage to *Raasay*, it was necessary to pass over a large part of *Sky*. We were furnished therefore with horses and a guide. In the islands there are no roads, nor any marks by which a stranger may find his way. The horseman has always at his side a native of the place, who, by pursuing game, or tending cattle, or being often employed in messages or conduct, has learned where the ridge of the hill has breadth sufficient to allow a horse and his rider a passage, and where the moss or bog is hard enough to bear them. The bogs are avoided as toilsome at least, if not unsafe, and therefore the journey is made generally from precipice to precipice; from which, if the eye ventures to look down, it sees below a gloomy cavity, whence the rush of water is sometimes heard.

But there seems to be in all this more alarm than danger. The Highlander walks carefully before, and the horse, accustomed to the ground, follows him with little deviation. Sometimes the hill is too steep for the horseman to keep his seat, and sometimes the moss is too tremulous to bear the double weight of horse and man. The rider then dismounts, and all shift as they can.

Journeys made in this manner are rather tedious than long. A

At the foot of 'Beinn na Caillich', all that remains now of Coire Chatachain where the two travellers found congenial if cramped hospitality. Boswell got slightly drunk but not so much so that he failed to notice that the minister, with whom he shared a bedroom, undressed in front of the maid and merely turned his back on her while he made water in the pot!

very few miles require several hours. From *Armidel* we came at night to Coriatachan, a house very pleasantly situated between two brooks, with one of the highest hills of the island behind it. It is the residence of Mr. *Mackinnon*, by whom we were treated with very liberal hospitality, among a more numerous and elegant company than it could have been supposed easy to collect.

The hill behind the house we did not climb. The weather was rough, and the height and steepness discouraged us. We were told that there is a cairne upon it. A cairne is a heap of stones thrown upon the grave of one eminent for dignity of birth, or splendour of achievements. It is said that by digging, an urn is always found under these cairnes; they must therefore have been thus piled by a people whose custom was to burn the dead. To pile stones is, I believe, a northern custom, and to burn the body was the Roman practice; nor do I know when it was that these two acts of sepulture were united.

The weather was next day too violent for the continuation of our journey; but we had no reason to complain of the interruption. We saw in every place, what we chiefly desired to know, the manners of the people. We had company, and, if we had chosen retirement, we might have had our books.

I never was in any house of the islands where I did not find books in more languages than one, if I staid long enough to want them, except one from which the family was removed. Literature is not neglected by the higher rank of the Hebrideans.

It need not, I suppose, be mentioned, that in countries so little frequented as the Islands, there are no houses where travellers are entertained for money. He that wanders about these wilds, either procures recommendations to those whose habitations lie near his way, or, when night and weariness come upon him, takes the chance of general hospitality. If he finds only a cottage, he can expect little more than shelter; for the cottagers have little more for themselves: but if his good fortune brings him to the residence of a gentleman, he will be glad of a storm to prolong his stay. There is, however, one inn by the sea-side at *Sconsor* in *Sky*, where the post-office is kept.

At the tables where a stranger is received, neither plenty nor delicacy is wanting. A tract of land so thinly inhabited, must have much wild-fowl; and I scarcely remember to have seen a dinner without them. The moorgame is everywhere to be had. That the sea abounds with fish, needs not be told, for it supplies a great part of Europe. The Isle of *Sky* has stags and roebucks, but no hares. They sell very numerous droves of oxen yearly to England, and therefore cannot be supposed to want beef at home. Sheep and goats are in great numbers, and they have the common domestic fowls.

But as here is nothing to be bought, every family must kill its own meat, and roast part of it somewhat sooner than Apicius would prescribe. Every kind of flesh is undoubtedly excelled by the variety and emulation of English markets; but that which is not best may be yet free from bad, and he that shall complain of his fare in the *Hebrides* has improved his delicacy more than his manhood.

Their fowls are not like those plumped for sale by the poulterers of London, but they are as good as other places commonly afford, except that the geese, by feeding in the sea, have universally a fishy rankness.

These geese seem to be of a middle race, between the wild and domestick kinds. They are so tame as to own a home, and so wild as sometimes to fly quite away.

Their native bread is made of oats, or barley. Of oatmeal they spread very thin cakes, coarse and hard, to which unaccustomed palates are not easily reconciled. The barley cakes are thicker and softer; I began to eat them without unwillingness; the blackness of their colour raises some dislike, but the taste is not disagreeable. In most houses there is wheat flower, with which we were sure to be treated if we stayed long enough to have it kneaded and baked. As neither yeast nor leaven are used among them, their bread of every kind is unfermented. They make only cakes and never mould a loaf.

A man of the Hebrides, for of the women's diet I can give no account, as soon as he appears in the morning, swallows a glass of whisky; yet they are not a drunken race, at least I never was present at much intemperance; but no man is so abstemious as to refuse the morning dram, which they call a *skalk.*

The word *whisky* signifies water, and is applied by way of eminence to *strong water*, or distilled liquor. The spirit drunk in the North is drawn from barley. I never tasted it, except once for experiment at the inn in *Inverary*, when I thought it preferable to any *English* malt brandy. It was strong, but not pungent, and was free from the empyreumatic taste or smell. What was the process I had no opportunity of inquiring, nor do I wish to improve the art of making poison pleasant.

Not long after the dram, may be expected the breakfast, a meal in which the Scots, whether of the lowlands or mountains, must be confessed to excel us. The tea and coffee are accompanied not only with butter, but with honey, conserves and marmalades. If an epicure could remove by a wish in quest of sensual gratifications, wherever he had supped he would breakfast in Scotland.

In the islands, however, they do what I found is not very easy to endure. They pollute the tea-table by plates piled with large slices of cheshire cheese, which mingles its less grateful odours with the fragrance of the tea.

Where many questions are to be asked, some will be omitted. I forgot to inquire how they were supplied with so much exotic luxury. Perhaps the French may bring them wine for wool, and the Dutch give them tea and coffee at the fishing season, in exchange for fresh provisions. Their trade is unconstrained; they pay no customs; for there is no officer to demand them; whatever therefore is made dear only by impost is obtained here at an easy rate.

A dinner in the Western Islands differs very little from a dinner in *England*, except that in the place of tarts, there are always set different preparations of milk. This part of their diet will admit some improvement. Though they have milk, and eggs, and sugar, few of them know how to compound them into a custard. Their gardens afford them no great variety, but they have always some vegetables on the table. Potatoes at least are never wanting, which, though they have not known them long, are now one of the principal parts of their food. They are not of the mealy, but the viscous kind.

Their more elaborate cookery, or made dishes, an Englishman, at the first taste is not likely to approve, but the culinary compositions of every country are often such as become grateful to other nations only by degrees; though I have read a French author, who, in the elation of his heart, says, that French cookery pleases all foreigners, but foreign cookery never satisfies a Frenchman.

Their suppers are, like their dinner, various and plentiful. The table is always covered with elegant linen. Their plates for common use are often of that kind of manufacture which is called cream coloured, or queen's ware. They use silver on all occasions where it is common in *England*, nor did I ever find the spoon of horn, but in one house.

The knives are not often either very bright, or very sharp. They are indeed instruments of which the Highlanders have not been long acquainted with the general use. They were not regularly laid on the table before the prohibition of arms, and the change of dress. Thirty years ago the Highlander wore his knife as a companion to his dirk or dagger, and when the company sat down to meat, the men who had knives cut the flesh into small pieces for the women, who with their fingers conveyed it to their mouths.

There was perhaps never any change of national manners so quick, so great, and so general, as that which has operated in the Highlands, by the last conquest, and the subsequent laws. We came thither too late to see what we expected, a people of peculiar appearance, and a system of antiquated life. The clans retain little now of their original character, their ferocity of temper is softened, their military ardour is extinguished, their dignity of independence is depressed, their contempt of government subdued, and their reverence for their chiefs abated. Of what they had before the late conquest of their country, there remain only their language and their poverty. Their language is attacked on every side. Schools are erected, in which *English* only is taught, and there were lately some who thought it reasonable to refuse them a version of the holy scriptures, that they might have no monument of their mother tongue.

That their poverty is gradually abated, cannot be mentioned

among the unpleasing consequences of subjection. They are now acquainted with money, and the possibility of gain will by degrees make them industrious. Such is the effect of the late regulations, that a longer journey than to the Highlands must be taken by him whose curiosity pants for savage virtues and barbarous grandeur.

Johnson sailed up the Sound of Raasay from Broadford. Now a vehicle ferry takes a few minutes to cross from Sconser to Raasay.

RAASAY

At the first intermission of the stormy weather we were informed, that the boat, which was to convey us to *Raasay*, attended us on the coast. We had from this time our intelligence facilitated, and our conversation enlarged, by the company of Mr. Macqueen, minister of a parish in *Sky*, whose knowledge and politeness give him a title equally to kindness and respect, and who, from this time, never forsook us till we were preparing to leave Sky and the adjacent places.

The boat was under the direction of Mr. *Malcolm Macleod*, a gentleman of *Raasay*. The water was calm, and the rowers were vigorous; so that our passage was quick and pleasant. When we came near the island, we saw the laird's house, a neat modern fabrick, and found Mr. *Macleod*, the proprietor of the Island, with many gentlemen, expecting us on the beach. We had, as at all other places, some difficulty in landing. The crags were irregularly broken, and a false step could have been very mischievous.

It seemed that the rocks might, with no great labour, have been hewn almost into a regular flight of steps; and as there are no other landing places, I considered this rugged ascent as the consequence of a form of life inured to hardships, and therefore not studious of nice accommodations. But I know not whether, for many ages, it was not considered as a part of military policy, to keep the country not easily accessible. The rocks are natural fortifications, and an enemy climbing with difficulty, was easily destroyed by those who stood high above him.

Our reception exceeded our expectations. We found nothing but civility, elegance, and plenty. After the usual refreshments, and the usual conversation, the evening came upon us. The carpet was then rolled off the floor; the musician was called, and the whole company was invited to dance, nor did ever fairies trip with greater alacrity. The general air of festivity, which predominated in this place, so far remote from all those regions which the mind has been used to contemplate as the mansions of pleasure, struck the imagination with a delightful surprise, analogous to that which is felt is an unexpected emersion from darkness into light.

When it was time to sup. the dance ceased, and six and thirty persons sat down to two tables in the same room. After supper the ladies sung *Erse* songs, to which I listened as an English audience to an *Italian* opera, delighted with the sound of words of which I did not understand.

I inquired the subjects of the songs, and was told of one, that it was a love song, and of another, that it was a farewell composed by one of the Islanders that was going, in this epidemical fury of emigration, to seek his fortune in America. What sentiments would rise on such an occasion, in the heart of one who had not been taught to lament by precedent, I should gladly have known; but the lady, by whom I sat, thought herself not equal to the work of translating.

Mr. *Macleod* is the proprietor of the islands of *Raasay*, *Rona*, and *Fladda*, and posssesses an extensive district in *Sky*. The estate has not, during four hundred years, gained or lost a single acre. He acknowledges Macleod of Dunvegan as his chief, though his ancestors have formerly disputed the pre-eminence.

One of the old Highland alliances has continued for two hundred years, and is still subsisting between *Macleod* of *Raasay* and *Macdonald* of *Sky*, in consequence of which the survivor always inherits the arms of the deceased; a natural memorial of military friendship. At the death of the late Sir *James Macdonald*, his sword was delivered to the present laird of *Raasay*.

The family of *Raasay* consists of the laird, the lady, three sons, and ten daughters. For the sons there is a tutor in the house, and the lady is said to be very skilful and diligent in the education of her girls. More gentleness of manners, or a more pleasing appearance of

domestick society, is not found in the most polished countries.

Raasay is the only inhabited island in Mr. *Macleod*'s possession. *Rona* and *Fladda* afford only pasture for cattle, of which one hundred and sixty winter in *Rona*, under the superintendence of a solitary herdsman.

The length of Raasay is, by computation, fifteen miles, and the breadth two. These countries have never been measured, and the computation by miles is negligent and arbitrary. We observed in travelling that the nominal and real distance of places had very little relation to each other. *Raasay* probably contains nearly a hundred square miles. It affords not much ground, notwithstanding its extent, either for tillage, or pasture; for it is rough, rocky, and barren. The cattle often perish by falling from the precipices. It is like the other islands, I think, generally naked of shade, but it is naked by neglect; for the laird has an orchard, and very large forest trees grow about his house. Like other hilly countries it has many rivulets. One of the brooks turns a corn-mill, and at least one produces trouts.

In the streams or fresh lakes of the islands, I have never heard of any other fish than trouts and eels. The trouts, which I have seen, are not large; the colour of their flesh is tinged as in *England*. Of their eels I can give no account, having never tasted them; for I believe they are not considered as wholesome food.

It is not very easy to fix the principles upon which mankind have agreed to eat some animals, and reject others; and as the principle

The mooring-place for the new ferry. Raasay has had chapters of sad history since Johnson's day. The good landlordism which Johnson admired so much disappeared when the descendant of his host, MacLeod of Raasay, had to sell the island and emigrate to Australia. The new purchaser promptly evicted about 120 families to make room for his sheep farms.

is not evident, it is not uniform. That which is selected as delicate in one country, is by its neighbours abhorred as loathsome. The Neapolitans lately refused to eat potatoes in a famine. An Englishman is not easily persuaded to dine on snails with an Italian, on frogs with a Frenchman, or on horse-flesh with a Tartar. The vulgar inhabitants of *Sky*, I know not whether of the other islands, have not only eels, but pork and bacon in abhorrence, and accordingly I never saw a hog in the *Hebrides*, except one at *Dunvegan*.

Raasay has wild fowl in abundance, but neither deer, hares, nor rabbits. Why it has them not, might be asked, but that of such questions there is no end. Why does any nation want what it might have? Why are not spices transplanted to *America*? Why does tea continue to be brought from China? Life improves but by slow degrees, and much in every place is yet to do. Attempts have been made to raise roebucks in *Raasay*, but without effect. The young ones it is extremely difficult to rear, and the old can very seldom be taken alive.

Hares and rabbits might be more easily obtained. That they have few or none of either in *Sky*, they impute to the ravage of the foxes, and have therefore set, for some years past, a price upon their heads, which, as the number was diminished, has been gradually raised from three shillings and sixpence to a guinea, a sum so great in this part of the world, that, in a short time, *Sky* may be as free from foxes, as *England* from wolves. The fund for these rewards is a tax of sixpence in the pound, imposed by the farmers on themselves, and said to be paid with great willingness.

The beasts of prey in the Islands are foxes, otters, and weasels. The foxes are bigger than those of *England*; but the otters exceed ours in a far greater proportion. I saw one at Armidel, of a size much beyond that which I supposed them ever to attain; and Mr. *Maclean*, the heir of Col, a man of middle stature, informed me that he once shot an otter, of which the tail reached the ground, when he held up the head to a level with his own. I expected the otter to have a foot particularly formed for the art of swimming; but upon examination, I did not find it differing much from that of a spaniel. As he preys in the sea, he does little visible mischief, and is killed only for his fur. White otters are sometimes seen.

In *Raasay* they might have hares and rabbits, for they have no foxes. Some depredations, such as were never made before, have caused a suspicion that a fox has been lately landed in the island by spite or wantonness. This imaginary stranger has never yet been seen, and therefore, perhaps, the mischief was done by some other animal. It is not likely a creature so ungentle, whose head could have been sold in Sky for a guinea, should be kept alive only to gratify the malice of sending him to prey upon a neighbour; and the passage from Sky is wider than a fox would venture to swim, unless he were chased by dogs into the sea, and perhaps then his strength

Glen Moriston. One of General Wade's forty bridges built after the Jacobite Rising of 1715.

BELOW
The house now standing on the site of the inn at Glenelg. When it was being restored by Mr Graham Noble in 1976 he found post-holes and oak beams dating the building back to the 1620s. The property was used by the garrison of Bernera Barracks between 1721 and 1820 and when Mr Noble was buying the building he found that the War Office still had pre-emption rights on it.

would enable him to cross. How beasts of prey came into any islands is not easy to guess. In cold countries they take advantage of hard winters, and travel over the ice: but this is a very scanty solution; for they are found where they have no discoverable means of coming.

The corn of this island is but little. I saw the harvest of a small field. The women reaped the corn, and the men bound up the sheaves. The strokes of the sickle were timed by the modulation of the harvest song, in which all their voices were united. They accompany in the Highlands every action which can be done in equal time, with an appropriate strain, which has, they say, not much meaning; but its effects are regularity and cheerfulness. The ancient proceleusmatic song, by which the rowers of galleys were animated, may be supposed to have been of this kind. There is now an *oar-song* used by the *Hebridians*.

The ground of *Raasay* seems fitter for cattle than for corn, and of black cattle I suppose the number is very great. The laird himself keeps a herd of four hundred, one hundred of which were annually sold. Of an extensive domain, which he holds in his own hands, he considers the sale of cattle as repaying him the rent, and supports the plenty of a very liberal table with the remaining product.

Raasay is supposed to have been very long inhabited. On one side of it they show caves, into which the rude natives of the first ages retreated from the weather. These dreary vaults might have had other uses. There is still a cavity near the house called the *oar-cave*, in which the seamen, after one of those piratical expeditions, which in rougher times was very frequent, used, as tradition tells, to hide their oars. This hollow was near the sea, that nothing so necessary might be far to be fetched; and it was secret, that enemies, if they landed, could find nothing. Yet it is not very evident of what use it was to hide their oars from those who, if they were masters of the coast, could take away their boats.

A proof much stronger of the distance at which the first possessors of this island lived from the present time, is afforded by the stone heads of arrows which are very frequently picked up. The people call them *Elf-bolts*, and believe that the fairies shoot them at the cattle. They nearly resemble those which Mr. *Banks* has lately brought from the savage countries in the Pacifick Ocean, and must have been made by a nation to which the use of metals was unknown.

The number of this little community has never been counted by its ruler, nor have I obtained any positive account, consistent with the result of political computation. Not many years ago, the late Laird led out one hundred men upon a military expedition. The sixth part of a people is supposed capable of bearing arms: *Raasay* had therefore six hundred inhabitants. But because it is not likely, that every man able to serve in the field would follow the summons, or that the chief would leave his lands totally defenceless, or take away all the hands qualified for labour, let it be supposed, that half

Raasay House (on the site of the one in which Johnson stayed) is now an adventure school.

as many might be permitted to stay at home. The whole number will then be nine hundred or nine to a square mile; a degree of populousness greater than those tracts of desolation can often show. They are content with their country, and faithful to their chiefs, and yet uninfected with the fever of migration.

Near the house at *Raasay*, is a chapel unroofed and ruinous, which has long been used only as a place of burial. About the churches, in the islands, are small squares inclosed with stones, which belong to particular families, as repositories for the dead. At *Raasay* there is one, I think, for the proprietor, and one for some collateral house.

It is told by *Martin*, that at the death of the Lady of the Island, it has been here the custom to erect a cross. This we found not to be true. The stones that stand about the chapel at a small distance, some of which perhaps have crosses cut upon them, are believed to have been not funeral monuments, but the ancient boundaries of the sanctuary or consecrated ground.

Martin was not a man illiterate: he was an inhabitant of *Sky*, and therefore was within reach of intelligence, and with no great difficulty might have visited the places which he undertakes to describe; yet with all his opportunities, he has often suffered himself to be deceived. He lived in the last century, when the chiefs of the clans had lost little of their original influence. The mountains were yet unpenetrated, no inlet was opened to foreign novelties, and the feudal institutions operated upon life with their full force. He might therefore have displayed a series of subordination and a form of government, which, in more luminous and improved regions, have been long forgotten, and have delighted his readers with many uncouth customs that are now disused, and wild opinions that prevail no longer. But he probably had not knowledge of the world

OPPOSITE ABOVE
A modern car ferry now connects Raasay with Sconser in Skye.

OPPOSITE BELOW
Raasay House, now an hotel.

RIGHT
Merchant Banker Iain Noble has founded a Gaelic College at Ostaig, and is trying to revitalise this historic part of Skye.

BELOW
The entrance to Armadale Castle, once the seat of the Chief of Macdonald. Now in the care of the Clan Donald Lands Trust. It houses the Clan Donald Centre.

sufficient to qualify him for judging what would deserve or gain the attention of mankind. The mode of life which was familiar to himself, he did not suppose unknown to others, nor imagined that he could give pleasure by telling that of which it was, in his little country, impossible to be ignorant.

What he has neglected cannot now be performed. In nations, where there is hardly the use of letters, what is once out of sight is lost for ever. They think but little, and of their few thoughts, none are wasted on the past, in which they are neither interested by fear nor hope. Their only registers are stated observances and practical representations. For this reason an age of ignorance is an age of ceremony. Pageants, and processions, and commemorations, gradually shrink away, as better methods come into use of recording events, and preserving rights.

It is not only in *Raasay* that the chapel is unroofed and useless; through the few islands which we visited, we neither saw nor heard of any house of prayer, except in *Sky*, that was not in ruins. The malignant influence of *Calvinism* has blasted ceremony and decency together; and if the remembrance of papal superstition is obliterated, the monuments of papal piety are likewise effaced.

It has been, for many years, popular to talk of the lazy devotion of the Romish clergy; over the sleepy laziness of men that erected churches, we may indulge our superiority with a new triumph, by comparing it with the fervid activity of those who suffer them to fall.

Of the destruction of churches, the decay of religion must in time be the consequence; for while the public acts of the ministry are now performed in houses, a very small number can be present; and as the greater part of the Islanders make no use of books, all must necessarily live in total ignorance who want the opportunity of vocal instruction.

From these remains of ancient sanctity, which are everywhere to be found, it has been conjectured, that, for the last two centuries, the inhabitants of the Islands have decreased in number. This argument, which supposes that the churches have been suffered to fall, only because they are no longer necessary, would have some force if the houses of worship still remaining were sufficient for the people. But since they have now no churches at all, these venerable fragments do not prove the people of former times to have been more numerous, but to have been more devout. If the inhabitants were doubled with their present principles, it appears not that any provision for publick worship would be made. Where the religion of a country enforces consecrated buildings, the number of those buildings may be supposed to afford some indication, however uncertain, of the populousness of the place; but where by a change of manners a nation is contented to live without them, their decay implies no diminution of inhabitants.

One of the satirical Rowlandson prints showing Boswell dancing on top of Duncaan Hill in Raasay.

Some of these dilapidations are said to be found in islands now uninhabited; but I doubt whether we can thence infer that they were ever peopled. The religion of the middle age is well known to have placed too much hope in lonely austerities. Voluntary solitude was the great art of propitiation, by which crimes were effaced, and conscience was appeased; it is therefore not unlikely, that oratories were often built in places where retirement was sure to have no disturbance.

Raasay has little that can detain a traveller, except the laird and his family; but their power wants no auxiliaries. Such a seat of hospitality, amidst the winds and waters, fills the imagination with a delightful contrariety of images. Without is the rough ocean and the rocky land, the beating billows and the howling storm: within is plenty and elegance, beauty and gaiety, the song and the dance. In *Raasay*, if I could have found an Ulysses, I had fancied a *Phaeacia*.

DUNVEGAN

At *Raasay*, by good fortune, *Macleod*, so the chief of the clan is called, was paying a visit, and by him we were invited to his seat at *Dunvegan*. Raasay has a stout boat, built in *Norway*, in which, with six oars, he conveyed us back to *Sky*. We landed at *Port Re*, so called, because *James* the Fifth of *Scotland*, who had the curiosity to visit the Islands, came into it. The port it made by an inlet of the sea, deep and narrow, where a ship lay waiting to dispeople *Sky*, by carrying the natives away to *America*.

In coasting *Sky*, we passed by the cavern in which it was the custom, as *Martin* relates, to catch birds in the night, by making a

RIGHT
After years of absentee landlordism and scandalous neglect strenuous efforts are being made to rejuvenate the once prosperous island of Raasay.

BELOW
Raasay. In the background is Duncaan Hill on which Boswell danced!

LEFT
Portree, the capital of Skye. In Johnson's day it had only one inn; now it is a beautiful and unspoilt tourist centre.

Portree in 1813. This most charming of Hebridean towns now has a population of more than 1,500 people, and it is the ideal touring centre for Skye.

fire at the entrance. This practice is disused; for birds, as is known often to happen, have changed their haunts.

Here we dined at a publick house, I believe the only inn of the island, and having mounted our horses, travelled in the manner already described till we came to *Kingsborough*, a place distinguished by that name because the King lodged here when he landed at Port Re. We were entertained with the usual hospitality by Mr. *Macdonald* and his lady, *Flora Macdonald*, a name that will be mentioned in history, and if courage and fidelity be virtues, mentioned with honour. She is a woman of middle stature, soft features, gentle manners, and elegant presence.

In the morning we sent our horses round a promontory to meet us, and spared ourselves part of the day's fatigue, by crossing an arm of the sea. We had at last some difficulty in coming to *Dunvegan*; for our way led over an extensive moor, where every step was to be taken with caution, and we were often obliged to alight, because the ground could not be trusted. In travelling this watery flat, I perceived that it had a visible declivity, and might without much expense or difficulty be drained. But difficulty and expense are relative terms, which have different meanings in different places.

To *Dunvegan* we came, very willing to be at rest, and found our fatigues amply recompensed by our reception. Lady *Macleod*, who had lived many years in *England*, was newly come hither with her son and four daughters, who knew all the arts of southern elegance, and all the modes of English economy. Here therefore we settled, and did not spoil the present hour with thoughts of departure.

Dunvegan is a rocky prominence, that juts out into a bay, on the west side of *Sky*. The house, which is the principal seat of Macleod,

The ruins of the old house of Kingsburgh can still be seen on the road (A 856) between Portree and Kilmuir. It was here that Prince Charlie spent the night having finally escaped 'over the sea to Skye' from the Western Isles. It was the home of Flora Macdonald and her husband, Allan, in 1773 and Johnson and Boswell spent the night there. Johnson makes very brief reference to their visit but Boswell found it very 'heady' in every sense of the word. However his hangover next morning did nothing to diminish his excitement at having shared with his idol the very room in which Prince Charlie had slept and the sight of seeing Dr Johnson lying in the tartan draped bed which had been Prince Charlie's struck Boswell 'with such a group of ideas as it is not easy for words to describe . . .' Johnson did not require many words to express his admiration for Flora; he noted Quantum cedet virtutibus aurum (How much less valuable than virtue is gold.)

The commemoration of Johnson's visit to Kingsburgh by the sketch of 'tea with Flora' (from Carruthers's edition of Boswell's Journal) gives a flimsy impression of the occasion. In actual fact the two visitors were extremely hospitably entertained by Flora Macdonald and her husband and she had immediately kittled the old man's sense of humour and endeared herself to him by saying that 'she had heard Mr Boswell was coming to Skye, and one Mr Johnson, a young English buck with him'. Although the Macdonalds were in dire financial straits and preparing to emigrate to America, a good dram of Holland's gin was followed by 'a genteel supper' which included an excellent roasted turkey, with porter to drink at table, and after supper claret and punch; of the latter, one suspects that Boswell drank Johnson's share as well as his own!

Johnson's 34-word tribute to Flora Macdonald sums up what generations of 'hagiographers' have attempted in reams of paper.

She was born in Milton, South Uist, in 1722 – the daughter of one of the better-off Macdonald tacksmen – and she met Prince Charlie when he was a hopeless fugitive in the Outer Hebrides with a price of £30,000 on his head. The Hebrides were virtually sealed off by Hanoverian troops and no amount of romantic brouhaha can do justice to the courage of a 24-year-old woman prepared to run the gauntlet of the Hanoverian forces, whose brutality was only too well known, in order to get Charles Edward Stuart across the Minch and on the route to safety. That is precisely what she did – disguising the Prince as her Irish maidservant – but while he escaped to France she was captured and imprisoned in London for eight months. However, the Government were too shrewd to martyr her and she was treated reasonably well and ultimately allowed to return home to Scotland.

Life in Skye was difficult during the upheavals following Culloden, and the year after Johnson's visit Flora and her family emigrated to America where, almost immediately, they got involved in the American Civil War and, ironically, raised a regiment of over 500 Highlanders to fight for the British Hanoverian Government! Her husband, who stayed on in America – after being captured during the War – in the hope of establishing a home and a living there, rejoined Flora in Skye in 1784 and was given Government compensation of £440.

OPPOSITE ABOVE
The north of Skye, which Johnson missed, has scenery that is surrealist to the point of appearing lunar!

OPPOSITE BELOW
Dunvegan Castle. After 800 years it is still the home of the Chief of MacLeod, although he spends much of his time in London.

LEFT
In the early days the sea-gate was the only entrance to Dunvegan fortress.

Dunvegan Castle in the early nineteenth century.

is partly old and partly modern; it is built upon the rock, and looks upon the water. It forms two sides of a small square: on the third side is the skeleton of a castle of unknown antiquity, supposed to have been a *Norwegian* fortress, when the Danes were masters of the Islands. It is so nearly entire, that it might have easily been made habitable, were there not an ominous tradition in the family, that the owner shall not long outlive the reparation. The grandfather of the present Laird, in defiance of prediction, began the work, but desisted in a little time, and applied his money to worse uses.

As the inhabitants of the *Hebrides* lived, for many ages, in continual expectation of hostilities, the chief of every clan resided in a fortress. This house was accessible only from the water, till the last possessor opened an entrance by stairs upon the land.

They had formerly reason to be afraid, not only of declared wars and authorised invaders, or of roving pirates, which, in the northern seas, must have been very common; but of inroads and insults from rival clans, who, in the plenitude of feudal independence, asked no leave of their Sovereign to make war on one another. *Sky* has been ravaged by a feud between the two mighty powers of *Macdonald* and *Macleod*. *Macdonald* having married a *Macleod*, upon some discontent dismissed her, perhaps because she had brought him no children. Before the reign of *James* the Fifth, a Highland laird made a trial of his wife for a certain time, and if she did not please him, he was then at liberty to send her away. This, however, must always have offended, and *Macleod* resenting the injury, whatever were its circumstances, declared, that the wedding had been solemnized without a bonfire, but that the separation should be better illuminated; and raising a little army set fire to the territories of *Macdonald*, who returned the visit, and prevailed.

Dunvegan Castle has been the home of the Chiefs of Clan MacLeod for an unbroken period of more than 700 years. In its early days the only entrance to it was by the Seagate because its communications were by sea with Rodel in Harris. Although the ancestral home is Dunvegan, the MacLeods are the MacLeods of Harris.

The Chiefs of MacLeod have an enviable record of caring for their clansfolk and maintaining the culture and tradition of the Highlands. Up till the end of the seventeenth century the Chief of MacLeod maintained a clan bard, a clan historian and a clan piper. It was in Dunvegan that the great MacCrimmon College of Piping was established and the piping tradition is maintained there to this day.

Shown here is the Great Hall (not very great by some standards!) which is a living museum of priceless clan treasures. Rory Mor's Cup is a silver chalice dating back to the tenth century; Rory Mor's drinking horn is a trophy won by Chief Malcolm in the fourteenth century for a bare-handed fight against a bull; the Fairy Flag (the most priceless treasure of all) was made of silk in the Far East more than a thousand years ago, and there are even those who would claim it was Christ's shirt; it

was brought back from the Crusades. The legend is that the flag has magic powers to save the Clan MacLeod from threatening disaster on the occasion of each of three unfurlings; it has been used twice already to good effect and it is supposed to have one more time to go. Strangely nobody thought of telling Johnson and Boswell of its existence, probably because nobody remembered; at that time it was locked away in an iron chest for safety, and some cynics maintain that its removal from the chest for the purposes of displaying it on the wall constituted the third unfurling. Hundreds of MacLeod servicemen carried postcard photographs of it as a talisman during the last war.

Rory Mor's horn is a drinking horn with a capacity of a bottle and two thirds of claret; to prove his manhood each presumptive heir to the Chiefship must down it at one draught on the occasion of his coming of age.

Old Dr Johnson was happy at Dunvegan; he would be flattered to know that his portrait has pride of place along with Clan Chief portraits on the wall of the Great Hall!

In Dunvegan Castle Dr Johnson slept in the bedroom of Sir Rory ('Mor') MacLeod (1562–1626), the greatest of the MacLeod Chiefs. The waterfall outside the window was supposed to have lulled the Chief to sleep and it was known as Rory Mor's nursemaid.

Another story may show the disorderly state of insular neighbourhood. The inhabitants of the Isle of *Egg*, meeting a boat manned by *Macleods*, tied the crew hand and foot, and set them adrift. *Macleod* landed upon *Egg*, and demanded the offenders; but the inhabitants refusing to surrender them, retreated to a cavern, into which they thought their enemies unlikely to follow them. *Macleod* choked them with smoke, and left them lying dead by families as they stood.

Here the violence of the weather confined us for some time, not at all to our discontent or inconvenience. We would indeed very willingly have visited the Islands, which might be seen from the house scattered in the sea, and I was particularly desirous to have viewed *Isay*; but the storms did not permit us to launch a boat, and we were condemned to listen in idleness to the wind, except when we were better engaged by listening to the ladies.

We had here more winds than waves, and suffered the severity of a tempest, without enjoying its magnificence. The sea being broken by the multitude of islands, does not roar with so much noise, nor beat the storm with such foamy violence, as I have remarked on the coast of *Sussex*. Though, while I was in the *Hebrides*, the wind was extremely turbulent, I never saw very high billows.

The country about *Dunvegan* is rough and barren. There are no trees, except in the orchard, which is a low sheltered spot surrounded with a wall.

When this house was intended to sustain a siege, a well was made in the court, by boring the rock downwards, till water was found, which, though so near to the sea, I have not heard mentioned as brackish, though it has some hardness or other qualities, which make it less fit for use, and the family is now better supplied from a stream, which runs by the rock, from two pleasing waterfalls.

Here we saw some traces of former manners, and heard some standing traditions. In the house is kept an ox's horn, hollowed so as to hold perhaps two quarts which the heir of Macleod was expected to swallow at one draught, as a test of his manhood, before he was permitted to bear arms or could claim a seat among the men. It is held, that the return of the laird to *Dunvegan*, after any considerable absence, produces a plentiful capture of herrings; and that, if any woman crosses the water to the opposite Island, the herrings will desert the coast. *Boethius* tells the same of some other place. The tradition is not uniform. Some hold that no woman may pass, and others that none may pass but a *Macleod*.

Among other guests, which the hospitality of Dunvegan brought to the table, a visit was paid by the Laird and Lady of a small island south of *Sky*, of which the proper name is *Muack*, which signifies swine. It is commonly called *Muck*, which the proprietor not liking, has endeavoured, without effect, to change to *Monk*. It is usual to call gentlemen in *Scotland* by the name of their possessions, as

John, the 23rd Chief of MacLeod, with Rory Mor's horn which he had to empty at one draught on his 21st birthday. He practised with water for several weeks before the event, and then with diluted claret till he was able to drink the whole lot neat! John is a professional singer and actor; he is married to the Hungarian pianist Melita Kolin and they give frequent recitals together. Although John has to live in London he regards Dunvegan very much as his home.

The Fairy Flag of Clan MacLeod now hangs framed on the wall of the Great Hall. In the 1920s it was examined by experts in the Victoria and Albert Museum who declared it to be silk from Syria or Rhodes and they came to the conclusion that it was a holy relic, probably a saint's shirt.

Raasay, Bernera, Loch Buy, a practice necessary in countries inhabited by clans, where all that live in the same territory have one name, and must be therefore discriminated by some addition. This gentleman, whose name, I think, is *Maclean*, should be regularly called *Muck*; but the appellation, which he thinks too coarse for his island, he would like still less for himself, and he is therefore addressed by the title of *Isle of Muck*.

This little island, however it be named, is of considerable value. It is two *English* miles long, and three quarters of a mile broad, and consequently contains only nine hundred and sixty *English* acres. It is chiefly arable. Half of this little dominion the Laird retains in his own hand, and on the other half, live one hundred and sixty persons, who pay their rent by exported corn. What rent they pay we were not told, and could not decently inquire. The proportion of the people to the land is such, as the most fertile countries do not commonly maintain.

The laird, having all his people under his immediate view, seems to be very attentive to their happiness. The devastation of the small-pox, when it visits places where it comes seldom, is well known. He has disarmed it of its terror at *Muack*, by inoculating eighty of his people. The expense was two shillings and sixpence a head. Many trades they cannot have among them, but upon occasion he fetches a smith from the Isle of *Egg*, and has a tailor from the main land, six times a year. This Island well deserved to be seen, but the Laird's absence left us no opportunity.

Every inhabited island has its appendant and subordinate islets. *Muck*, however small, has yet others smaller about it, one of which has only ground sufficient to afford pasture for three wethers.

At *Dunvegan* I had tasted lotus, and was in danger of forgetting that I was ever to depart, till Mr. Boswell sagely reproached me with my sluggishness and softness. I had no very forcible defence to make, and we agreed to pursue our journey. *Macleod* accompanied us to *Ulinish*, where we were entertained by the sheriff of the Island.

ULINISH

Mr. *Macqueen* travelled with us, and directed our attention to all that was worthy of observation. With him we went to see an ancient building, called a dun or borough. It was a circular inclosure, about forty-two feet in diameter, walled round with loose stones, perhaps to the height of nine feet. The walls are very thick, diminishing a little towards the top, and though in these countries, stone is not brought far, must have been raised with much labour. Within the great circle were several smaller rounds of wall, which formed distinct apartments. Its date and its use are unknown. Some suppose it the original seat of the chiefs of the *Macleods*. Mr *Macqueen* thought it a *Danish* fort.

The entrance is covered with flat stones, and is narrow, because it was necessary that the stones which lie over it, should reach from one wall to the other; yet, straight as the passage is, they seem heavier than could have been placed where they now lie, by the naked strength of as many men as might stand about them. They were probably raised by putting long pieces of wood under them, to which the action of a long line of lifters might be applied. Savages, in all countries, have patience proportionate to their unskilfulness, and are content to attain their end by very tedious methods.

If it was ever roofed, it might once have been a dwelling, but as there is no provision for water, it could not have been a fortress. In *Sky*, as in every other place, there is an ambition of exalting whatever has survived memory, to some important use, and referring it to very remote ages. I am inclined to suspect, that in lawless times, when the inhabitants of every mountain stole the cattle of their neighbour, these enclosures were used to secure the herds and flocks in the night. When they were driven within the wall, they might be easily watched, and defended as long as could be needful; for the robbers durst not wait till the injured clan should find them in the morning.

The interior enclosures, if the whole building were once a house, were the chambers of the chief inhabitants. If it were a place of security for cattle, they were probably the shelters for the keepers.

From the *Dun* we were conducted to another place of security, a cave carried a great way under ground, which had been discovered by digging after a fox. These caves, of which many have been found, and many probably remain concealed, are formed, I believe, commonly by taking advantage of a hollow, where banks or rocks rise on either side. If no such place can be found, the ground must be cut away. The walls are made by piling stones against the earth, on either side. It is then roofed by large stones laid across the cavern, which therefore cannot be wide. Over the roof, turfs were placed, and grass was suffered to grow; and the mouth was concealed by bushes, or some other cover.

These caves were represented to us as the cabins of the first rude inhabitants, of which, however, I am by no means persuaded. This was so low, that no man could stand upright in it. By their construction they are all so narrow, that two can never pass along them together, and being subterraneous, they must be always damp. They are not the work of an age much ruder than the present; for they are formed with as much art as the construction of a common hut requires. I imagine them to have been places only of occasional use, in which the Islander, upon a sudden alarm, hid his utensils, or his clothes, and perhaps sometimes his wife and children.

This cave we entered, but could not proceed the whole length, and went away without knowing how far it was carried. For this omission we shall be blamed, as we perhaps have blamed other travellers; but the day was rainy, and the ground was damp. We had with us neither spades nor pickaxes, and if love of ease surmounted our desire of knowledge, the offence has not the invidiousness of singularity.

Edifices, either standing or ruined, are the chief records of an illiterate nation. In some part of this journey, at no great distance from our way, stood a shattered fortress, of which the learned minister, to whose communication we are much indebted, gave us an account.

Those, said he, are the walls of a place of refuge, built in the time of James the Sixth, by Hugh Macdonald, who was next heir to the dignity and fortune of his chief. Hugh, being so near his wish, was impatient of delay; and had art and influence sufficient to engage several gentlemen in a plot against the Laird's life. Something must be stipulated on both sides; for they would not dip their hands in blood merely for Hugh's advancement. The compact was formally written, signed by the conspirators, and placed in the hands of one Macleod.

It happened that Macleod had sold some cattle to a drover who, not having ready money, gave him a bond for payment. The debt was discharged, and the bond redemanded, which Macleod, who could not read, intending to put into his hands, gave him the conspiracy. The drover, when he had read the paper, delivered it privately to Macdonald, who, being thus informed of his danger, called his friends together, and provided for his safety. He made a public feast, and inviting Hugh Macdonald and his confederates, placed each of them at the table between two men of known fidelity. The compact of conspiracy was then shewn, and every man confronted with his own name. Macdonald acted with great moderation. He upbraided Hugh, both with disloyalty and ingratitude; but told the rest, that he considered them as men deluded and misinformed. Hugh was sworn to fidelity, and dismissed with his companions; but he was not generous enough to be reclaimed by lenity; and finding no longer any countenance among the gentlemen, endeavoured to execute the same design by meaner hands. In this practice he was detected, taken to Macdonald's castle, and imprisoned in the dungeon. When he was hungry, they let down a plentiful meal of salted meat; and when, after his repast, he called for drink, conveyed to him a covered cup, which, when he lifted the lid, he found empty. From that time they visited him no more, but left him to perish in solitude and darkness.

We were told of a cavern by the sea-side remarkable for the powerful reverberation of sounds. After dinner we took a boat to explore this curious cavity. The boatmen, who seemed to be of a rank above common drudges, inquired who the strangers were, and being told we came one from *Scotland*, and the other from *England*, asked if the *Englishman* could recount a long genealogy. What answer was given them, the conversation being in *Erse*, I was not much inclined to examine.

They expected no good event of the voyage; for one of them declared that he heard the cry of an *English* ghost. This omen I was not told till after our return, and therefore cannot claim the dignity of despising it.

The sea was smooth. We never left the shore, and came without any disaster to the cavern, which we found rugged and misshapen, about one hundred and eighty feet long, thirty wide in the broadest part, and in the loftiest, as we guessed, about thirty high. It was now dry, but at high water the sea rises in it near six feet. Here I saw what I had never seen before, limpets and mussels in their natural state. But, as a new testimony to the veracity of common fame, here was no echo to be heard.

We then walked through a natural arch in the rock, which might have pleased us by its novelty, had the stones, which encumbered our feet, given us leisure to consider it. We were shown the gummy seed of the kelp, that fastens itself to a stone, from which it grows into a strong stalk.

In our return, we found a little boy upon the point of a rock, catching with his angle, a supper for the family. We rowed up to him, and borrowed his rod, with which Mr. Boswell caught a cuddy.

The cuddy is a fish of which I know not the philosophical name. It is not much bigger than a gudgeon, but is of great use in these Islands, as it affords the lower people both food, and oil for their lamps. Cuddies are so abundant, at some times of the year, that they are caught like white-bait in the Thames only by dipping a basket and drawing it back.

If it were always practicable to fish, these islands could never be in much danger from famine; but unhappily in the winter, when other provision fails, the seas are commonly too rough for nets, or boats.

TALISKER IN SKY

From *Ulinish*, our next stage was to *Talisker*, the house of colonel *Macleod*, an officer in the *Dutch* service, who in this time of universal peace, has for several years been permitted to be absent from his regiment. Having been bred to physick he is consequently a scholar, and his lady, by accompanying him in his different places of residence, is becoming skilful in several languages. *Talisker* is the place, beyond all that I have seen, from which the gay and the jovial seem utterly excluded; and where the hermit might expect to grow old in meditation, without possibility of disturbance or interruption. It is situated very near the sea, but upon a coast where no vessel lands but when it is driven by a tempest on the rocks. Towards the land are lofty hills streaming with water-falls. The garden is sheltered by firs, or pines, which grow there so prosperously, that some, which the present inhabitant planted, are very high and thick.

At this place we very happily met Mr. *Donald Maclean*, a young gentleman, the eldest son of the Laird of *Col*, heir to a very great extent of land, and so desirous of improving his inheritance, that he spent a considerable time among the farmers of *Hertfordshire*, and *Hampshire*, to learn their practice. He worked with his own hands at the principal operations of agriculture, that he might not deceive himself by a false opinion of skill, which if he should find it deficient at home, he had no means of completing. If the world has agreed to praise the travels and manual labours of the Czar of *Muscovy*, let *Col* have his share of the like applause, in the proportion of his dominions to the empire of *Russia*.

This young gentleman was sporting in the mountains of *Sky*, and when he was weary with following his game, repaired for lodging to *Talisker*. At night he missed one of his dogs, and when he went to seek him in the morning, found two eagles feeding on his carcass.

Col, for he must be named by his possessions, hearing that our intention was to visit *Iona*, offered to conduct us to his chief, Sir *Allan Maclean*, who lived in the Isle of *Inch Kenneth*, and would readily find us a convenient passage. From this time was formed an acquaintance, which being begun by kindness, was accidentally continued by constraint; we derived much pleasure from it, and I hope have given him no reason to repent it.

The weather was now almost one continued storm, and we were to snatch some happy intermission to be conveyed to *Mull*, the third Island of the Hebrides, lying about a degree south of *Sky*, whence we might easily find our way to *Inch Kenneth*, where Sir *Allan Maclean* resided, and afterwards to *Iona*.

For this purpose, the most commodious station that we could take was *Armidel*, which Sir *Alexander Macdonald* had now left to a gentleman, who lived there as his factor or steward.

On our way to Armidel, was Coriatachan, where we had already been, and to which therefore we were very willing to return. We stayed however so long at Talisker, that a great part of our journey was performed in the gloom of the evening. In travelling even thus almost without light through naked solitude, when there is a guide whose conduct may be trusted, a mind not naturally too much disposed to fear, may preserve some degree of cheerfulness; but what must be the solicitude of him who should be wandering, among the crags and hollows, benighted, ignorant, and alone?

The fictions of the *Gothick* romances were not so remote from credibility as they are now thought. In the full prevalence of the feudal institution, when violence desolated the world, and every baron lived in a fortress, forests and castle were regularly succeeded by each other, and the adventurer might very suddenly pass from the gloom of woods, or the ruggedness of moors, to seats of plenty, gaiety, and magnificence. Whatever is imaged in the wildest tale, if giants, dragons, and enchantment be excepted, would be felt by him, who, wandering in the mountains without a guide, or upon the sea without a pilot, should be carried amidst his terrour and uncertainty, to the hospitality and elegance of *Raasay* or *Dunvegan*.

To Coriatachan at last we came, and found ourselves welcomed as before. Here we stayed two days, and made such inquiries as curiosity suggested. The house was filled with company, among whom Mr. *Macpherson* and his sister distinguished themselves by their politeness and accomplishments. By him we were invited to *Ostig*, a house not far from Armidel, where we might easily hear of a boat, when the weather would suffer us to leave the island.

OSTIG IN SKY

At *Ostig*, of which Mr. *Macpherson* is minister, we were entertained for some days, then removed to *Armidel*, where we finished our observations on the island of *Sky*.

As this Island lies in the fifty-seventh degree, the air cannot be supposed to have much warmth. The long continuance of the sun above the horizon does indeed sometimes produce great heat in northern latitudes; but this can only happen in sheltered places, where the atmosphere is to a certain degree stagnant, and the same mass of air continues to receive for many hours the rays of the sun, and the vapours of the earth. *Sky* lies open on the west and north to a vast extent of ocean, and is cooled in the summer by a perpetual ventilation, but by the same blasts is kept warm in winter. Their weather is not pleasing. Half the year is deluged with rain. From the autumnal to the vernal equinox, a dry day is hardly known, except when the showers are suspended by a tempest. Under such skies can be expected no great exuberance of vegetation. Their winter overtakes their summer, and their harvest lies upon the ground drenched with rain. The autumn struggles hard to produce some of

When the Clan Donald estates in Skye were sold to meet death duties in 1971, 22,000 acres were bought by Iain Noble who was determined to revitalize the decaying economy of Sleat while preserving the traditional way of life. Noble is the antithesis of the absentee landlord. He lives in Skye and travels from there to attend to his worldwide business interests. His sincerity has won him the confidence of local people who have well founded distrust of landlords, and he has succeeded in inspiring a certain degree of confidence. His hotel and his various local enterprises are staffed by Gaelic speakers.

Iain Noble is a passionate believer in the future of the Gaelic language given the right economic and social conditions. He learnt the language himself and is a fluent speaker. His greatest triumph in Skye has been the establishment of a Gaelic College in a restored barn in Ostaig (or 'Ostig' as Johnson called it). Sabhal Mor Ostaig (to give it its Gaelic title) now has the backing of the Scottish Education Department and of the Regional Councils of the Highlands and the Western Isles. In addition to various courses for learners of Gaelic it now offers a diploma course (conducted in Gaelic) in economic and business studies in conjunction with Stirling University. Johnson would enjoy a return visit to Ostig *— and perhaps does . . . who knows!*

our early fruits. I gathered gooseberries in September; but they were small, and the husk was thick.

Their winter is seldom such as puts a full stop to the growth of plants, or reduces the cattle to live wholly on the surplusage of the summer. In the year Seventy-one they had a severe season, remembered by the name of the Black Spring, from which the island has not yet recovered. The snow lay long upon the ground, a calamity hardly known before. Part of their cattle died for want, part were unseasonably sold to buy sustenance for the owners; and, what I have not read or heard of before, the kine that survived were so emaciated and dispirited that they did not require the male at the usual time. Many of the roebucks perished.

The soil, as in other countries, has its diversities. In some parts there is only a thin layer of earth spread upon a rock, which bears nothing but short brown heath, and perhaps is not generally capable of any better product. There are many bogs or mosses of greater or less extent where the soil cannot be supposed to want depth, though it is too wet for the plough. But we did not observe in these any aquatick plants. The vallies and the mountains are alike darkened with heath. Some grass, however, grows here and there, and some happier spots of earth are capable of tillage.

The crooked spade tillage to which Johnson refers. This photograph was taken by Jon Wyand at the Auchindrain Museum in Argyll.

Their agriculture is laborious, and perhaps rather feeble than unskilful. Their chief manure is seaweed, which, when they lay it to rot upon the field, gives them a better crop than those of the Highlands. They heap sea-shells upon the dunghill, which in time moulder into a fertilizing substance. When they find a vein of earth where they cannot use it, they dig it up, and add it to the mould of a more commodious place.

Their corn grounds often lie in such intricacies among the craggs, that there is no room for the action of a team and plough. The soil is then turned up by manual labour, with an instrument called a crooked spade, of a form and weight which to me appeared very incommodious, and would perhaps be soon improved in a country where workmen could be easily found and easily paid. It has a narrow blade of iron fixed to a long and heavy piece of wood, which must have, about a foot and a half above the iron, a knee or flexure with the angle downwards. When the farmer encounters a stone which is the great impediment of his operations, he drives the blade under it, and bringing the knee or angle to the ground, has in the long handle a very forcible lever.

According to the different mode of tillage, farms are distinguished into *long land* and *short land*. Long land is that which affords room for a plough, and short land is turned up by the spade.

The grain which they commit to the furrows, thus tediously formed, is either oats or barley. They do not sow barley without very copious manure, and then they expect from it ten for one, an increase equal to that of better countries; but the culture is so operose that they content themselves commonly with oats; and who can relate without compassion, that after all their diligence they are to expect only a triple increase? It is in vain to hope for plenty, when a third part of the harvest must be reserved for seed.

When their grain is arrived at the state which they must consider as ripeness, they do not cut, but pull the barley: to the oats they apply a sickle. Wheel carriages they have none, but make a frame of timber, which is drawn by one horse with the two points behind pressing on the ground. On this they sometimes drag home their sheaves, but often convey them in a kind of open panier, or frame of sticks upon the horse's back.

Of that which is obtained with so much difficulty, nothing surely ought to be wasted; yet their method of clearing their oats from the husk is by parching them in the straw. Thus, with the genuine improvidence of savages, they destroy that fodder for want of which their cattle may perish. From this practice they have two petty conveniencies. They dry the grain so that it is easily reduced to meal, and they escape the theft of the thresher. The taste contracted from the fire by the oats, as by every other scorched substance, use must long ago have made grateful. The oats that are not parched must be dried in a kiln.

The barns of *Sky* I never saw. That which *Macleod* and *Raasay* had erected near his house was so contrived, because the harvest is seldom brought home dry, as by perpetual perflation to prevent the mow from heating.

Of their gardens I can judge only from their tables. I did not observe that the common greens were wanting, and suppose, that by choosing an advantageous exposition, they can raise all the more hardy esculent plants. Of vegetable fragrance or beauty they are not yet studious. Few vows are made to Flora in the *Hebrides*.

They gather a little hay, but the grass is mown late; and is so often almost dry and again very wet, before it is housed, that it becomes a collection of withered stalks, without taste or fragrance; it must be eaten by cattle that having nothing else, but by most English farmers would be thrown away.

In the Islands I have not heard that any subterraneous treasures have been discovered, though where there are mountains, there are commonly minerals. One of the rocks in *Col* has a black vein, imagined to consist of the ore of lead; but it was never yet opened or essayed. In *Sky* a black mass was accidentally picked up, and brought into the house of the owner of the land, who found himself strongly inclined to think it a coal, but unhappily it did not burn in the chimney. Common ores would be here of no great value; for what requires to be separated by fire, must, if it were found, be carried away in its mineral state, here being no fewel for the smelting-house, or forge. Perhaps by diligent search in this world of stone, some valuable species of marble might be discovered. But

The Highland economy up till the middle of the eighteenth century was based on black cattle. Johnson refers to the droving of the cattle to the mainland markets like Falkirk. Such a drove was re-enacted (although with a slightly different type of beast) in 1981. In this photograph by Graham Noble the drove is preparing to swim the narrows from Skye to Glenelg.

neither philosophical curiosity, nor commercial industry, have yet fixed their abode here, where the importunity of immediate want supplied but for the day, and craving on the morrow, has left little room for excursive knowledge, or the pleasing fancies of distant profit.

They have lately found a manufacture considerably lucrative. Their rocks abound with kelp, a sea plant, of which the ashes are melted into glass. They burn kelp in great quantities, and then send it away in ships, which come regularly to purchase them. This new source of riches has raised the rents of many maritime farms; but the tenants pay, like all other tenants, the additional rent with great unwillingness; because they consider the profits of the kelp as the mere product of personal labour, to which the landlord contributes nothing. However, as any man may be said to give what he gives the power of gaining, he has certainly as much right to profit from the price of kelp as anything else found or raised upon his ground.

This new trade has excited a long and eager litigation between *Macdonald* and *Macleod*, for a ledge of rocks, which, till the value of kelp was known, neither of them desired the reputation of possessing.

The cattle of *Sky* are not so small as is commonly believed. Since they have sent their beeves in great numbers to southern marts, they have probably taken more care of their breed. At stated times the annual growth of cattle is driven to a fair, by a general drover, and with the money, which he returns to the farmer, the rents are paid.

The price regularly expected is from two to three pounds a head; there was once one sold for five pounds. They go from the island very lean, and are not offered to the butcher, till they have been long fatted in *English* pastures.

Of their black cattle, some are without horns, called by the Scots *humble* cows, as we call a bee an *humble* bee, that wants a sting. Whether this difference be specific or accidental, though we inquired with great diligence, we could not be informed. We are not very sure that the bull is ever without horns, though we have been told that such bulls there are. What is produced by putting a horned and unhorned male and female together, no man has ever tried that thought the result worthy of observation.

Their horses are, like their cows, of a moderate size. I had no difficulty to mount myself commodiously by the favour of the gentlemen. I heard of very little cows in *Barra*, and very little horses in *Rum*, where perhaps no care is taken to prevent that diminution of size, which must always happen when the greater and the less copulate promiscuously, and the young animal is restrained from growth by penury of sustenance.

The goat is the general inhabitant of the earth, complying with every difference of climate and of soil. The goats of the *Hebrides* are like others: nor did I hear anything of their sheep to be particularly remarked.

In the penury of these malignant regions, nothing is left that can be converted to food. The goats and the sheep are milked like the cows. A single meal of a goat is a quart, and of a sheep a pint. Such at least was the account, which I could extract from those of whom I am not sure that they ever had inquired.

The milk of goats is much thinner than that of cows, and that of sheep is much thicker. Sheeps milk is never eaten before it is boiled: as it is thick, it must be very liberal of curd, and the people of *St. Kilda* form it into small cheeses.

The stags of the mountains are less than those of our parks, or forests, perhaps not bigger than our fallow deer. Their flesh has no rankness, nor is it inferior in flavour to our common venison. The roebuck I neither saw nor tasted. These are not countries for a regular chase. The deer are not driven with horns and hounds. A sportsman, with his gun in his hand, watches the animal, and, when he has wounded him, traces him by the blood.

They have a race of brindled greyhounds larger and stronger than those with which we course hares, and those are the only dogs used by them for the chase.

Man is by the use of fire-arms made so much an overmatch for other animals, that in all countries, where they are in use, the wild part of the creation sensibly decreases. There will probably not be long either stags or roebucks in the Islands. All the beasts of chase would have been lost long ago in countries well inhabited, had they not been preserved by laws for the pleasure of the rich.

There are in *Sky* neither rats nor mice, but the weasel is so frequent, that he is heard in houses rattling behind chests or beds, as rats in *England*. They probably owe to his predominance that they have no other vermin; for, since the great rat took possession of this part of the world, scarce a ship can touch at any port, but some of his race are left behind. They have within these few years began to infest the isle of *Col*, where being left by some trading vessel, they have increased for want of weasels to oppose them.

The inhabitants of *Sky*, and of the other Islands, which I have seen, are commonly of the middle stature, with fewer among them very tall or very short, than are seen in *England*, or perhaps, as their numbers are small, the chances of any deviation from the common measure are necessarily few. The tallest men that I saw are among those of higher rank. In regions of barrenness and scarcity, the human race is hindered in its growth by the same causes as other animals.

The ladies have as much beauty here as in other places, but bloom and softness are not to be expected among the lower classes, whose faces are exposed to the rudeness of the climate, and whose features are sometimes contracted by want, and sometimes hardened by the blasts. Supreme beauty is seldom found in cottages or work-shops, even where no real hardships are suffered. To expand the human face to its full perfection, it seems necessary that the mind should co-operate by placidness of content, or consciousness of superiority.

Their strength is proportionate to their size, but they are accustomed to run upon rough ground, and therefore can with great agility skip over the bog or clamber the mountain. For a campaign in the wastes of *America* soldiers better qualified could not have been found. Having little work to do, they are not willing nor perhaps able to endure a long continuance of manual labour, and are therefore considered as habitually idle.

Having never been supplied with these accommodations, which life extensively diversified with trades affords, they supply their wants with very insufficient shifts, and endure many inconveniences which a little attention would easily relieve. I have seen a horse carrying home the harvest on a crate. Under his tail was a stick for a crupper, held at the two ends by twists of straw. Hemp will grow in their islands, and therefore ropes may be had. If they wanted hemp, they might make better cordage of rushes, or perhaps of nettles, than of straw.

Their method of life neither secures them perpetual health, nor exposes them to any particular diseases. There are physicians in the Islands, who I believe, all practise chirurgery, and all compound their own medicines.

It is generally supposed, that life is longer in places where there are few opportunities of luxury; but I found no instance here of extraordinary longevity. A cottager grows old over his oaten cakes, like a citizen at a turtle feast. He is indeed seldom incommoded by corpulence. Poverty preserves him from sinking under the burden of himself, but he escapes no other injury of time. Instances of long life are often related, which those who hear them are more willing to credit than examine. To be told that any man has attained a hundred years, gives hope and comfort to him who stands trembling on the brink of his own climacterick.

Length of life is distributed impartially to very different modes of life in very different climates; and the mountains have no greater examples of age and health than the low lands, where I was introduced to two ladies of high quality; one of whom, in her ninety-fourth year, presided at her table with the full exercise of all her powers; and the other has attained her eighty-fourth, without any diminution of her vivacity, and with little reason to accuse time of depredations on her beauty.

In the Islands, as in most other places, the inhabitants are of different rank, and one does not encroach here upon another. Where there is no commerce nor manufacture, he that is born poor can scarcely become rich; and if none are able to buy estates, he that is born to land cannot annihilate his family be selling it. This was once the state of these countries. Perhaps there is no example, till within a century and a half, of any family whose estate was alienated otherwise than by violence or forfeiture. Since money has been brought amongst them, they have found, like others, the art of spending more than they receive; and I saw with grief the chief of a very ancient clan, whose Island was condemned by law to be sold for the satisfaction of his creditors.

The name of highest dignity is Laird, of which there are in the extensive Isle of *Sky* only three, *Macdonald*, *Macleod*, and *Mackinnon*. The Laird is the original owner of the land, whose natural power must be very great, where no man lives but by agriculture; and where the produce of the land is not conveyed through the labyrinths of traffick, but passes directly from the hand that gathers it to the mouth that eats it. The Laird has all those in his power that live upon his farms. Kings can, for the most part, only exalt or degrade. The Laird at pleasure can feed or starve, can give bread, or withhold it. This inherent power was strengthened by the kindness of consanguinity, and the reverence of patriarchal authority. The Laird was the father of the Clan, and his tenants commonly bore his name. And to these principles of original command was added, for many ages, an exclusive right of legal jurisdiction.

This multifarious and extensive obligation operated with force scarcely credible. Every duty, moral or political, was absorbed in affection and adherence to the Chief. Not many years have passed since the Clan knew no law but the Laird's will. He told them to whom they should be friends or enemies, what king they should obey, and what religion they should profess.

When the Scots rose in arms against the succession of the house of *Hanover*, *Lovat*, the Chief of the Frasers, was in exile for a rape. The Frasers were very numerous, and very zealous against the government. A pardon was sent to *Lovat*. He came to the *English* camp, and the Clan immediately deserted to him.

Next in dignity to the Laird is the Tacksman, a large taker or lease-holder of land, of which he keeps part, as a domain in his own hand, and lets part to under-tenants. The Tacksman is necessarily a man capable of securing to the laird the whole rent, and is commonly a collateral relation. These *tacks*, or subordinate possessions, were long considered as hereditary, and the occupant was distinguished by the name of the place at which he resided. He held a middle station, by which the highest and the lowest orders were connected. He paid rent and reverence to the Laird, and received them from the tenants. This tenure still subsists, with its original operation, but not with the primitive stability. Since the islanders, no longer content to live, have learned the desire of growing rich, an ancient dependent is in danger of giving way to a higher bidder, at the expense of domestick dignity and hereditary power. The stranger, whose money buys him preference, considers himself as paying for all that he has, and is indifferent about the Laird's honour or safety. The commodiousness of money is indeed great; but there are some advantages which money cannot buy, and which therefore no wise man will by the love of money be tempted to forego.

I have found in the hither parts of *Scotland*, men not defective in judgment or general experience, who consider the Tacksman as a useless burden of the ground, as a drone who lives upon the product of an estate, without the right of property, or the merit of labour, and who impoverishes at once the landlord and the tenant. The land, say they, is let to the Tacksman at six-pence an acre, and by him to the tenant at ten-pence. Let the owner be the immediate landlord to all the tenants; if he sets the ground at eight-pence, he will increase his revenue by a fourth part, and the tenant's burden will be diminished by a fifth.

Those who pursue this train of reasoning, seem not sufficiently to inquire whither it will lead them, nor to know that it will equally show the propriety of suppressing all wholesale trade, of shutting up the shops of every man who sells what he does not make, and of extruding all whose agency and profit intervene between the manufacturer and the consumer. They may, by stretching their understandings a little wider, comprehend, that all those who by undertaking large quantities of manufacture, and affording employment to many labourers, make themselves considered as benefactors to the publick, have only been robbing their workmen with one hand, and their customers with the other. If Crowley had sold only what he could make, and all his smiths had wrought their own iron with their own hammers, he would have lived on less, and they would have sold their work for more. The salaries of superintendents and clerks would have been partly saved, and partly shared, and nails been sometimes cheaper by a farthing in a hundred. But then if the smith could not have found an immediate purchaser, he must have deserted his anvil; if there had by accident at any time been more sellers than buyers, the workmen must have reduced their profit to nothing, by underselling one another; and as no great stock could have been in any hand, no sudden demand of large quantities could have been answered, and the builder must have stood still till the nailer could supply him.

According to these schemes, universal plenty is to begin and end in universal misery. Hope and emulation will be utterly extinguished; and as all must obey the call of immediate necessity, nothing that requires extensive views, or provides for distant consequences, will ever be performed.

To the southern inhabitants of Scotland, the state of the mountains and the islands is equally unknown with that of *Borneo* or *Sumatra*; Of both they have only heard a little, and guess the rest. They are strangers to the language and the manners, to the advantages and wants of the people, whose life they would model, and whose evils they would remedy.

Nothing is less difficult than to procure one convenience for the forfeiture of another. A soldier may expedite his march by throwing away his arms. To banish the Tacksman is easy, to make a country plentiful by diminishing the people is an expeditious mode of husbandry; but that abundance, which there is nobody to enjoy, contributes little to human happiness.

As the mind must govern the hands, so in every society the man of intelligence must direct the man of labour. If the Tacksmen be taken away, the Hebrides must in their present state be given up to grossnesss and ignorance; the tenant for want of admonition will be negligent. The Laird, in these wide estates, which often consist of islands remote from one another, cannot extend his personal influence to all his tenants; and the steward having no dignity annexed to his character, can have little authority among men taught to pay reverence only to birth, and who regard the Tacksman as their hereditary superior; nor can the steward have equal zeal for the prosperity of an estate profitable only to the Laird, with the Tacksman, who has the laird's income involved in his own.

The only gentlemen in the islands are the Lairds, the Tacksmen, and the Ministers, who frequently improve their livings by becoming farmers. If the Tacksmen be banished, who will be left to impart knowledge or impress civility? The Laird must always be at a distance from the greater part of his lands; and if he resides at all upon them, must drag his days in solitude, having no longer either a friend or a companion; he will therefore depart to some more comfortable residence, and leave the tenants to the wisdom and mercy of a factor.

Of tenants there are different orders, as they have greater or less stock. Land is sometimes leased to a small fellowship, who live in a cluster of huts, called a Tenants Town, and are bound jointly and

The ruins of the White House of Grissipol on the island of Coll.

separately for the payment of their rent. These, I believe, employ in the care of their cattle, and the labour of tillage, a kind of tenants yet lower; who having a hut, with grass for a certain number of cows and sheep, pay their rent by a stipulated quantity of labour.

The condition of domestick servants, or the price of occasional labour, I do not know with certainty. I was told that the maids have sheep, and are allowed to spin for their own clothing; perhaps they have no pecuniary wages, or none but in very wealthy families. The state of life which has hitherto been purely pastoral, begins now to be a little variegated with commerce; but novelties enter by degrees, and till one mode has fully prevailed over the other, no settled notion can be formed.

Such is the system of insular subordination, which, having little variety, cannot afford much delight in the view, nor long detain the mind in contemplation. The inhabitants were for a long time perhaps not unhappy; but their content was a muddy mixture of pride and ignorance, an indifference for pleasures they did not know, a blind veneration for their chiefs, and a strong conviction of their own importance.

Their pride has been crushed by the heavy hand of a vindictive conqueror, whose severities have been followed by laws, which, though they cannot be called cruel, have produced much discontent, because they operate upon the surface of life, and make every eye bear witness to subjection. To be compelled to a new dress has always been found painful.

Their chiefs being now deprived of their jurisdiction, have already lost much of their influence; and as they gradually degenerate from patriarchal rulers to rapacious landlords, they will divest themselves of the little that remains.

That dignity which they derived from an opinion of their military importance, the law, which disarmed them, has abated. An old gentleman, delighting himself with the recollection of better days, related, that forty years ago, a Chieftain walked out attended by ten or twelve followers, with their arms rattling. That animating rabble has now ceased. The Chief has lost his formidable retinue; and the Highlander walks his heath unarmed and defenceless, with the peaceable submission of a French peasant or English cottager.

Their ignorance grows every day less, but their knowledge is yet of little other use than to show them their wants. They are now in the period of education, and feel the uneasiness of discipline, without yet perceiving the benefit of instruction.

The last law, by which the Highlanders are deprived of their arms, has operated with efficacy beyond expectation. Of former statutes made with the same design, the execution has been feeble, and the effect inconsiderable. Concealment was undoubtedly practised, and perhaps often with connivance. There was tenderness or partiality on one side, and obstinacy on the other. But the law which followed the victory of Culloden, found the whole nation dejected and intimidated; informations were given without danger, and without fear, and the arms were collected with such rigour, that every house was despoiled of its defence.

To disarm part of the Highlands, could give no reasonable occasion of complaint. Every government must be allowed the power of taking away the weapon that is lifted against it. But the loyal clans murmured, with some appearance of justice, that after having defended the King, they were forbidden for the future to defend themselves; and that the sword should be forfeited, which had been legally employed. Their case is undoubtedly hard, but in political regulations, good cannot be complete, it can only be predominant.

Whether by disarming a people thus broken into several tribes, and thus remote from the seat of power, more good than evil has been produced, may deserve inquiry. The supreme power in every community has the right of debarring every individual, and every subordinate society, from self-defence, only because the supreme power is able to defend them; and therefore where the governor cannot act, he must trust the subject to act for himself. These Islands might be wasted with fire and sword before their sovereign would know their distress. A gang of robbers, such as has been lately found confederating themselves in the Highlands, might lay a wide region under contribution. The crew of a petty privateer might land on the largest and most wealthy of the Islands, and riot without control in cruelty and waste. It was observed by one of the Chiefs of *Sky*, that fifty armed men might, without resistance, ravage the country. Laws that place the subjects in such a state, contravene the first principles of the compact of authority: they exact obedience, and yield no protection.

It affords a generous and manly pleasure to conceive a little nation gathering its fruits and tending its herds with fearless confidence, though it lies open on every side to invasion, where, in contempt of walls and trenches, every man sleeps securely with his sword beside him; where all on the first approach of hostility came together at the call to battle, as at a summons to a festal show; and committing their cattle to the care of those whom age or nature has disabled, engage the enemy with that competition for hazard and for glory, which operate in men that fight under the eye of those, whose dislike or kindness they have always considered as the greatest evil or the greatest good.

This was, in the beginning of the present century, the state of the Highlands. Every man was a soldier, who partook of national confidence, and interested himself in national honour. To lose this spirit is to lose what no small advantage will compensate.

It may likewise deserve to be inquired, whether a great nation ought to be totally commercial? Whether, amidst the uncertainty of human affairs, too much attention to one mode of happiness may

RIGHT
*Breachdachaidh Castle on Coll
dates back to the fourteenth
century.*

Mull is overpowering in its beauty and desolation. Emigration and eviction and absentee landlordism have wrought havoc in this potentially prosperous island of the Inner Hebrides.

OPPOSITE

Tobermory in the island of Mull. Like various other West Highland villages it was designed as a fishing station during attempts to resuscitate the Highland economy at the end of the tragic eighteenth century. Tobermory is one of the best anchorages in Scotland and a haven for yachts; the Tobermory Regatta is held in early August and attracts yachts from the whole west coast of Scotland. The harbour proved unsafe for one vessel – the Florencia, *reputedly a treasure ship of the Spanish Armada which was blown up while seeking shelter there in 1588. She is now the property of the Dukes of Argyll who try to raise her from time to time – or, at least, raise some of her vast riches.*

not endanger others? Whether the pride of riches must not sometimes have recourse to the protection of courage? And whether, if it be necessary to preserve in some part of the empire the military spirit, it can subsist more commodiously in any place, than in remote and unprofitable provinces, where it can commonly do little harm, and whence it may be called forth at any sudden exigence?

It must, however, be confessed, that a man who places honour only in successful violence, is a very troublesome and pernicious animal in time of peace; and that the martial character cannot prevail in a whole people, but by the diminution of all other virtues. He that is accustomed to resolve all right into conquest, will have very little tenderness or equity. All the friendship in such a life can be only a confederacy of invasion, or alliance of defence. The strong must flourish by force, and the weak subsist by stratagem.

Till the Highlanders lost their ferocity, with their arms, they suffered from each other all that malignity could dictate, or precipitance could act. Every provocation was revenged with blood, and no man that ventured into a numerous company, by whatever occasion brought together, was sure of returning without a wound. If they are now exposed to foreign hostilities, they may talk of the danger, but can seldom feel it. If they are no longer martial, they are no longer quarrelsome. Misery is caused for the most part, not by a heavy crush of disaster, but by the corrosion of less visible evils, which canker enjoyment and undermine security. The visit of an invader is necessarily rare, but domestick animosities allow no cessation.

The abolition of the local jurisdictions, which had for so many ages been exercised by the Chiefs, has likewise its evil and its good. The feudal constitution naturally diffused itself into long ramifications of subordinate authority. To this general temper of the government was added the peculiar form of the country, broken by mountains into many sub-divisions scarcely accessible but to the natives, and guarded by passes, or perplexed with intricacies, through which national justice could not find its way.

The power of deciding controversies, and of punishing offences, as some such power there must always be, was entrusted to the Lairds of the country, to those whom the people considered as their natural judges. It cannot be supposed that a rugged proprietor of the rocks, unprincipled and unenlightened, was a nice resolver of entangled claims, or very exact in proportioning punishment to offences. But the more he indulged his own will, the more he held his vassals in dependence. Prudence and innocence, without the favour of the Chief, conferred no security; and crimes involved no danger when the judge was resolute to acquit.

When the chiefs were men of knowledge and virtue, the convenience of a domestick judicature was great. No long journies were necessary, nor artificial delays could be practised; the character, the alliances and interests of the litigants were known to the court, and all false pretences were easily detected. The sentence, when it was past, could not be evaded; the power of the Laird superseded formalities, and justice could not be defeated by interest or stratagem.

I doubt not but that since the regular judges have made their circuits through the whole country, right has been every where more wisely and more equally distributed; the complaint is, that litigation has grown troublesome, and that the magistrates are too few, and therefore often too remote for general convenience.

Many of the smaller Islands have no legal officer within them. I once asked, If a crime should be committed, by what authority the offender could be seized; and was told, that the laird would exert his right; a right which he must now usurp, but which surely necessity must vindicate, and which is therefore yet exercised in lower degrees, by some of the proprietors, when legal processes cannot be obtained.

In all greater questions, however, there is now happily an end to all fear or hope from malice or from favour. The roads are secure in those places through which, forty years ago, no traveller could pass without a convoy. All trials of right by the sword are forgotten, and the mean are in as little danger from the powerful as in other places. No scheme of policy has, in any country, yet brought the rich and poor on equal terms into courts of judicature. Perhaps experience, improving on experience, may in time effect it.

Those who have long enjoyed dignity and power, ought not to lose it without some equivalent. There was paid to the Chiefs by the publick, in exchange for their privileges, perhaps a sum greater than most of them had ever possessed, which excited a thirst for riches, of which it showed them the use. When the power of birth and station ceases, no hope remains but from the prevalence of money. Power and wealth supply the place of each other. Power confers the ability of gratifying our desire without the consent of others. Wealth enables us to obtain the consent of others to our gratification. Power, simply considered, whatever it confers on one, must take from another. Wealth enables its owner to give to others, by taking only from himself. Power pleases the violent and proud: wealth delights the placid and the timorous. Youth therefore flies at power, and age grovels after riches.

The Chiefs, divested of their prerogatives, necessarily turned their thoughts to the improvement of their revenues, and expect more rent, as they have less homage. The tenant, who is far from perceiving that his condition is made better in the same proportion, as that of his landlord is made worse, does not immediately see why his industry is to be taxed more heavily than before. He refuses to pay the demand, and is ejected; the ground is then let to a stranger, who perhaps brings a larger stock, but who, taking the land at its full price, treats with the Laird upon equal terms, and considers

The island of Ulva was the territory of the Clan Macquarrie. Lachlan Macquarie was a boy in Ulva when Johnson was there. As General Macquarie he succeeded the notorious Captain Bligh in Australia as Governor General of New South Wales. The Macquarie River and various other Australian places are named after him.

The Old Nunnery in Iona. Iona now belongs to the National Trust for Scotland, except for the Abbey which is the property of the Church of Scotland.

ABOVE
*Iona Abbey was restored by the
Iona Community under the
inspired leadership of Dr George
F. MacLeod, now Lord MacLeod
of Fiunary.*

LEFT
*Thousands of pilgrim tourists
worship in the restored Iona
Abbey. Although it belongs to the
Church of Scotland it is
interdenominational.*

him not as a Chief, but as a trafficker in land. Thus the estate perhaps is improved, but the Clan is broken.

It seems to be the general opinion, that the rents have been raised with too much eagerness. Some regard must be paid to prejudice. Those who have hitherto paid but little, will not suddenly be persuaded to pay much, though they can afford it. As ground is gradually improved, and the value of money gradually decreases, the rent may be raised without any diminution of the farmer's profits: yet it is necessary in these countries, where the ejection of a tenant is a greater evil, than in more populous places, to consider not merely what the land will produce, but with what ability the inhabitant can cultivate it. A certain stock can allow but a certain payment; for if the land be doubled, and the stock remains the same, the tenant becomes no richer. The proprietors of the Highlands might perhaps often increase their income, by subdividing the farms, and allotting to every occupier only so many acres as he can profitably employ, but that they want people.

There seems now, whatever be the cause, to be through a great part of the Higlands a general discontent. That adherence, which was lately professed by every man to the Chief of his name, has now little prevalence; and he that cannot live as he desires at home, listens to the tale of fortunate islands, and happy regions, where every man may have land of his own, and eat the product of his labour without a superior.

Those who have obtained grants of American lands, have, as is well known, invited settlers from all quarters of the globe; and among other places, where oppression might produce a wish for new habitations, their emissaries would not fail to try their persuasions in the Isles of Scotland, where at the time when the Clans were newly disunited from their Chiefs, and exasperated by unprecedented exactions, it is no wonder that they prevailed.

Whether the mischief of emigration were immediately perceived, may be justly questioned. They who went first, were probably such as could best be spared; but the accounts sent by the earliest adventurers, whether true or false, inclined many to follow them; and whole neighbourhoods formed parties for removal; so that departure from their native country is no longer exile. He that goes thus accompanied, carries with him all that makes life pleasant. He sits down in a better climate, surrounded by his kindred and his friends: they carry with them their language, their opinions, their popular songs, and hereditary merriment; they change nothing but the place of their abode; and of that change they perceive the benefit.

This is the real effect of emigration, if those that go away together settle on the same spot, and preserve their ancient union. But some relate that these adventurous visitants of unknown regions, after a voyage, passed in dreams of plenty and felicity, are dispersed at last upon a sylvan wilderness, where their first years must be spent in toil, to clear the ground which is afterwards to be tilled, and that the whole effect of their undertaking is only more fatigue and equal scarcity.

Both accounts may be suspected. Those who are gone will endeavour by every art to draw others after them; for as their numbers are greater, they will provide better for themselves. When *Nova Scotia* was first peopled, I remember a letter, published under the character of a New Planter, who related how much the climate put him in mind of Italy. Such intelligence the *Hebridians* probably receive from their transmarine correspondents. But with equal temptations of interest, and perhaps with no greater niceness of veracity, the owners of the Islands spread stories of American hardships to keep their people content at home.

Some method to stop this epidemick desire of wandering, which spreads its contagion from valley to valley, deserves to be sought with great diligence. In more fruitful countries, the removal of one, only makes room for the succession of another: but in the *Hebrides*, the loss of an inhabitant leaves a lasting vacuity; for nobody born in any other parts of the world will choose this country for his residence; and an Island once depopulated will remain a desert, as long as the present facility of travel gives every one, who is discontented and unsettled, the choice of his abode.

Let it be inquired, whether the first intention of those who are fluttering on the wing, and collecting a flock that they may take their flight, be to attain good, or to avoid evil. If they are dissatisfied with that part of the globe, which their birth has allotted them, and resolve not to live without the pleasures of happier climates; if they long for bright suns, and calm skies, and flowery fields, and fragrant gardens, I know not by what eloquence they can be persuaded, or by what offers they can be hired, to stay.

But if they are driven from their native country by positive evils, and disgusted by ill-treatment, real or imaginary, it were fit to remove their grievances, and quiet their resentment; since, if they have been hitherto undutiful subjects, they will not much mend their principles by American conversation.

To allure them into the army, it was thought proper to indulge them in the continuance of their national dress. If this concession could have any effect, it might easily be made. That dissimilitude of appearance, which was supposed to keep them distinct from the rest of the nation, might disincline them from coalescing with the *Pensylvanians* or people of *Connecticut*. If the restitution of their arms will reconcile them to their country, let them have again those weapons, which will not be more mischievous at home than in the colonies. That they may not fly from the increase of rent, I know not whether the general good does not require that the landlords be, for a time, restrained in their demands, and kept quiet by pensions proportionate to their loss.

RIGHT
*64 kings (from four different
countries) are alleged to lie buried
in Iona; among them are MacBeth
and King Duncan.*

OPPOSITE
*Grim Lochbuie Castle had been
abandoned in Johnson's day.*

BELOW
*Martyrs' Bay on the west coast of
Iona. Here, Columba landed from
Ireland in 563.*

The Clan MacLeod Parliament in session at Dunvegan in 1978, presided over by Chief John MacLeod of MacLeod. Under the chapter heading 'Ostig in Sky' Dr Johnson meditates at length on the evils and possible outcomes of the waves of emigration and eviction which were then just beginning to swell in the Highlands and might seed new Clans in the other hemisphere.

He was not far wrong. In the maritime provinces of Canada in particular, but also in New Zealand and Australia, the emigrant Highlanders tended to band together – bonded initially by common language, kinship and territorial origins – and while they may not have established new clans they certainly established new communities founded on old traditions. Today Gaelic is still the everyday language of many enclaves in Nova Scotia. As the bitterness gave way to sentiment (not always as mawkish as some critics make out) Clan Societies began to form all over the world, and they began to establish contact with the areas of their ancestral roots. One Chief who could afford to look back on her lineage with an easier conscience than most was the redoubtable Dame Flora MacLeod of MacLeod, the 28th Chief, who died in 1978. Her slogan was 'The word clan *means* children of the Chief *and Dunvegan Castle is your spiritual home,' and she did indeed strive to make Dunvegan a focal centre of interest, and a tartan Mecca for members of Clan MacLeod of whom there are 20,000 in the United States alone. To that end she established a Clan MacLeod Parliament which means every four years in Dunvegan under the chairmanship of the Chief with delegates drawn from almost every country in the Western world.*

To hinder insurrection by driving away the people, and to govern peaceably by having no subjects, is an expedient that argues no great profundity of politicks. To soften the obdurate, to convince the mistaken, to mollify the resentful, are worthy of a statesman; but it affords a legislator little self-applause to consider that, where there was formerly an insurrection, there is now a wilderness.

It has been a question often agitated without solution, why those northern regions are now so thinly peopled, which formerly overwhelmed with their armies the Roman empire. The question supposes what I believe is not true, that they had once more inhabitants than they could maintain, and overflowed only because they were full.

This is to estimate the manners of all countries and ages by our own. Migration, while the state of life was unsettled, and there was little communication of intelligence between distant places, was among the wilder nations of Europe, capricious and casual. An adventurous projector heard of a fertile coast unoccupied, and led out a colony; a chief of renown for bravery, called the young men together, and led them out to try what fortune would present. When Cæsar was in *Gaul*, he found the Helvetians preparing to go they knew not whither, and put a stop to their motions. They settled again in their own country, where they were so far from wanting room, that they had accumulated three years provision for their march.

The religion of the North was military; if they could not find enemies, it was their duty to make them; they travelled in quest of danger, and willingly took the chance of Empire or Death. If their troops were numerous, the countries from which they were collected are of vast extent, and without much exuberance of people great armies may be raised where every man is a soldier. But their true numbers were never known. Those who were conquered by them are their historians, and shame may have excited them to say, that they were overwhelmed with multitudes. To count is a modern practice, the ancient method was to guess; and when numbers are guessed they are always magnified.

Thus England has for several years been filled with the achievements of seventy thousand Highlanders employed in *America*. I have heard from an English officer, not much inclined to favour them, that their behaviour deserved a very high degree of military praise; but their number has been much exaggerated. One of the ministers told me, that seventy thousand men could not have been found in all the Highlands, and that more than twelve thousand never took the field. Those that went to the American war, went to destruction. Of the old Highland regiment, consisting of twelve hundred, only seventy-six survived to see their country again.

The Gothick swarms have at least been multiplied with equal liberality. That they bore no great proportion to the inhabitants, in whose countries they settled, is plain from the paucity of northern words now found in the provincial languages. Their country was not deserted for want of room, because it was covered with forests of vast extent; and the first effect of plenitude of inhabitants is the destruction of wood. As the Europeans spread over *America*, the lands are gradually laid naked.

I would not be understood to say, that necessity had never any part in their expeditions. A nation, whose agriculture is scanty or unskilful, may be driven out by famine. A nation of hunters may have exhausted their game. I only affirm that the northern regions were not, when their irruptions subdued the Romans, overpeopled with regard to their real extent of territory and power of fertility. In a country fully inhabited, however afterward laid waste, evident marks will remain of its former populousness. But of *Scandinavia* and *Germany*, nothing is known but that as we trace their state upwards into antiquity, their woods were greater and their cultivated ground was less.

That causes very different from want of room may produce a general disposition to seek another country, is apparent from the present conduct of the Highlanders, who are in some places ready to threaten a total secession. The numbers which have already gone, though like other numbers they may be magnified, are very great, and such as if they had gone together and agreed upon any certain settlement, might have founded an independent government in the depths of the western continent. Nor are they only the lowest and most indigent; many men of considerable wealth have taken with them their train of labourers and dependants; and if they continue the feudal scheme of polity, may establish new Clans in the other hemisphere.

'In this country every man is a MacLean', wrote Johnson. He got the spelling wrong. The Maclaines of Lochbuie are of the same descent as the Macleans of Duart, but each is a clan in its own right.

That the immediate motives of their desertion must be imputed to their landlords, may be reasonably concluded, because some Lairds of more prudence and less rapacity have kept their vassals undiminished. From *Raasay* only one man had been seduced, and at *Col* there was no wish to go away.

The traveller who comes hither from more opulent countries, to speculate upon the remains of pastoral life, will not much wonder that a common Highlander has no strong adherence to his native soil; for of animal enjoyments, or of physical good, he leaves nothing that he may not find again wheresoever he may be thrown.

The habitations of men in the *Hebrides* may be distinguished into huts and houses. By a *house*, I mean a building with one story over another; by a *hut*, a dwelling with only one floor. The Laird, who formerly lived in a castle, now lives in a house; sometimes sufficiently neat, but seldom very spacious or splendid. The tacksmen and the ministers have commonly houses. Wherever there is a house, the stranger finds a welcome; and to the other evils of exterminating tacksmen may be added the unavoidable cessation of hospitality, or the devolution of too heavy a burden on the ministers.

Of the houses, little can be said. They are small, and by the necessity of accumulating stores, where there are so few opportunities of purchase, the rooms are very heterogeneously filled. With want of cleanliness it were ingratitude to reproach them. The servants, having been bred upon the naked earth, think every floor clean, and the quick succession of guests, perhaps not always over-elegant, does not allow much time for adjusting their apartments.

Huts are of many gradations; from murky dens to commodious dwellings.

The wall of a common hut is always built without mortar, by a skilful adaptation of loose stones. Sometimes perhaps a double wall of stones is raised, and the intermediate space filled with earth. The air is thus completely excluded. Some walls are, I think, formed of turfs, held together by a wattle, or texture of twigs. Of the meanest huts, the first room is lighted by the entrance, and the second by the smoke-hole. The fire is usually made in the middle. But there are huts, or dwellings, of only one story, inhabited by gentlemen, which have walls cemented with mortar, glass windows, and boarded floors. Of these all have chimneys, and some chimneys have grates.

The house and the furniture are not always nicely suited. We were driven once, by missing a passage, to the hut of a gentleman, where, after a very liberal supper, when I was conducted to my chamber, I found an elegant bed of Indian cotton, spread with fine sheets. The accommodation was flattering; I undressed myself, and felt my feet in the mire. The bed stood upon the bare earth, which a long course of rain had softened to a puddle.

In pastoral countries the condition of the lowest rank of people is sufficiently wretched. Among manufacturers, men that have no property may have art and industry, which make them necessary, and therefore valuable. But where flocks and corn are the only wealth, there are always more hands than work, and of that work there is little in which skill and dexterity can be much distinguished. He therefore who is born poor never can be rich. The son merely occupies the place of the father, and life knows nothing of progression or advancement.

The petty tenants, and labouring peasants live in miserable cabins, which afford them little more than shelter from the storms. The Boor of *Norway* is said to make all his own utensils. In the *Hebrides*, whatever might be their ingenuity, the want of wood leaves them no materials. They are probably content with such accommodations as stones of different forms and sizes can afford them.

Their food is not better than their lodging. They seldom taste the flesh of land animals; for here are no markets. What each man eats is from his own stock. The great effect of money is to break property into small parts. In towns, he that has a shilling may have a piece of meat; but where there is no commerce, no man can eat mutton but by killing a sheep.

Fish, in fair weather, they need not want; but, I believe, man never lives long on fish, but by constraint; he will rather feed upon roots and berries.

The only fewel of the Islands is peat. Their wood is all consumed, and coal they have not yet found. Peat is dug out of the marshes, from the depth of one foot to that of six. That is accounted the best which is nearest the surface. It appears to be a mass of black earth held together by vegetable fibres. I know not whether the earth be bituminous, or whether the fibres be not the only combustible part; which, by heating the interposed earth red hot, make a burning mass. The heat is not very strong nor lasting. The ashes are yellowish, and in a large quantity. When they dig peat, they cut it into square pieces, and pile it up to dry beside the house. In some places it has an offensive smell. It is like wood charked for the smith. The common method of making peat fires, is by heaping it on the hearth; but it burns well in grates, and in the best houses is so used.

The common opinion is that peat grows again where it has been cut; which, as it seems to be chiefly a vegetable substance, is not unlikely to be true, whether known or not to those who relate it.

There are water mills in *Sky* and *Raasay*; but where they are too far distant, the housewives grind their oats with a quern, or handmill, which consists of two stones, about a foot and a half in diameter; the lower is a little convex, to which the concavity of the upper must be fitted. In the middle of the upper stone is a round hole, and on one side is a long handle. The grinder sheds the corn gradually into the hole with one hand, and works the handle round with the other. The corn slides down the convexity of the lower stone, and by the motion of the upper is ground in its passage. These stones are found in *Lochabar*.

The Islands afford few pleasures, except to the hardy sportsman, who can tread the moor and climb the mountain. The distance of one family from another, in a country where travelling has so much difficulty, makes frequent intercourse impracticable. Visits last several days, and are commonly paid by water; yet I never saw a boat furnished with benches, or made commodious by any addition to the first fabric. Conveniencies are not missed where they never were enjoyed.

The solace which the bagpipe can give, they have long enjoyed; but among other changes, which the last revolution introduced, the use of the bagpipe begins to be forgotten. Some of the chief families still entertain a piper, whose office was anciently hereditary. *Macrimmon* was piper to *Macleod*, and *Rankin* to *Maclean* of *Col*.

The tunes of the bagpipe are traditional. There has been in *Sky*, beyond all time of memory, a college of pipers, under the direction of Macrimmon, which is not quite extinct. There was another in *Mull*, superintended by *Rankin*, which expired about sixteen years ago. To these colleges, while the pipe retained its honour, the students of musick repaired for education. I have had my dinner exhilarated by the bagpipe, at *Armidel*, at *Dunvegan*, and in *Col*.

The general conversation of the Islanders has nothing particular. I did not meet with the inquisitiveness of which I have read, and suspect the judgment to have been rashly made. A stranger of curiosity comes into a place where a stranger is seldom seen; he importunes the people with questions, of which they cannot guess the motive, and gazes with surprise on things which they, having had them always before their eyes, do not suspect of anything wonderful. He appears to them like some being of another world, and then thinks it peculiar that they take their turn to inquire whence he comes, and whither he is going.

The Islands were long unfurnished with instruction for youth, and none but the sons of gentlemen could have any literature. There are now parochial schools, to which the lord of every manor pays a certain stipend. Here the children are taught to read; but by the rule of their institution, they teach only *English*, so that the natives read a language which they may never use or understand. If a parish, which often happens, contains several Islands, the school being but in one, cannot assist the rest. This is the state of *Col*, which, however, is more enlightened than some other places; for the deficiency is supplied by a young gentleman, who for his own improvement, travels every year on foot over the Highlands to the session at Aberdeen; and at his return, during the vacation, teaches to read and write in his native Island.

In *Sky* there are two grammar schools, where boarders are taken to be regularly educated. The price of board is from three pounds to four pounds ten shillings a year, and that of instruction is half a crown a quarter. But the scholars are birds of passage, who live at school only in the summer, for in winter provisions cannot be made for any considerable number in one place. This periodical dispersion impresses strongly the scarcity of these countries.

Having heard of no boarding-school for ladies nearer than *Inverness*, I suppose their education is generally domestick. The elder daughters of the higher families are sent into the world, and may contribute by their acquisitions to the improvement of the rest.

Women must here study to be either pleasing or useful. Their deficiencies are seldom supplied by very liberal fortunes. A hundred pounds is a portion beyond the hope of any but the Laird's daughter. They do not indeed often give money with their daughters; the question is, How many cows a young lady will bring her husband? A rich maiden has from ten to forty; but two cows are a decent fortune for one who pretends to no distinction.

The religion of the islands is that of the Kirk of *Scotland*. The gentlemen with whom I conversed are all inclined to the *English* liturgy; but they are obliged to maintain the established Minister, and the country is too poor to afford payment to another, who must live wholly on the contribution of his audience.

They therefore all attend the worship of the Kirk, as often as a visit from their Minister, or the practicability of travelling gives them opportunity; nor have they any reason to complain of insufficient pastors; for I saw not one in the Islands, whom I had reason to think either deficient in learning, or irregular in life; but found several with whom I could not converse without wishing, as my respect increased, that they had not been Presbyterians.

The ancient rigour of puritanism is now very much relaxed, though all are not yet equally enlightened. I sometimes met with prejudices sufficiently malignant, but they were prejudices of ignorance. The Ministers in the Islands had attained such knowledge as may justly be admired in men, who have no motive to study, but generous curiosity, or, what is still better, desire of usefulness; with such politeness as so narrow a circle of converse could not have supplied, but to minds naturally disposed to elegance.

Reason and truth will prevail at last. The most learned of the Scottish Doctors would now gladly admit a form of prayer, if the people would endure it. The zeal or rage of congregations has its different degrees. In some parishes the Lord's Prayer is suffered: in others it is still rejected as a form; and he that should make it part of his supplication would be suspected of heretical pravity.

The principle upon which extemporary prayer was originally introduced, is no longer admitted. The Minister formerly, in the effusion of his prayer, expected immediate, and perhaps perceptible inspiration, and therefore thought it his duty not to think before what he should say. It is now universally confessed, that men pray as they speak on other occasions, according to the general measure of their abilities and attainments. Whatever each may think of a form prescribed by another, he cannot but believe that he can himself compose by study and meditation a better prayer than will rise in his mind at a sudden call; and if he has any hope of supernatural help, why may he not as well receive it when he writes as when he speaks?

In the variety of mental powers, some must perform extemporary prayers with much imperfection; and in the eagerness and rashness of contradictory opinions, if publick liturgy be left to the private judgment of every Minister, the congregation may often be offended or misled.

There is, in Scotland, as among ourselves, a restless suspicion of popish machinations, and a clamour of numerous converts to the Romish religion. The report is, I believe, in both parts of the Island equally false. The Romish religion is professed only in *Egg* and *Canna*, two small islands, into which the Reformation never made its way. If any missionaries are busy in the Highlands, their zeal entitles them to respect, even from those who cannot think favourably of their doctrine.

The political tenets of the Islanders I was not curious to investigate, and they were not eager to obtrude. Their conversation is decent and inoffensive. They disdain to drink for their principles, and there is no disaffection at their tables. I never heard a health offered by a Highlander that might not have circulated with propriety within the precincts of the King's palace.

Legal government has yet something of novelty to which they cannot perfectly conform. The ancient spirit that appealed only to the sword, is yet among them. The tenant of *Scalpa*, an island belonging to Macdonald, took no care to bring his rent; when the landlord talked of exacting payment, he declared his resolution to keep his ground, and drive all intruders from the Island, and continued to feed his cattle as on his own land, till it became necessary for the Sheriff to dislodge him by violence.

The various kinds of supestition which prevailed here, as in all other regions of ignorance, are, by the diligence of the Ministers, almost extirpated.

Of *Browny* mentioned by Martin, nothing has been heard for many years. *Browny* was a sturdy Fairy; who, if he was well fed, and kindly treated, would, as they said, do a great deal of work. They now pay him no wages, and are content to labour for themselves.

In *Troda*, within these three-and-thirty years, milk was put every Saturday for *Greogach*, or *the Old Man with the Long Beard*. Whether *Greogach* was courted as kind, or dreaded as terrible, whether they meant, by giving him the milk, to obtain good, or avert evil, I was not informed. The Minister is now living by whom the practice was abolished.

They share still among them a great number of charms for the cure of different diseases; they are all invocations, perhaps transmitted to them from the times of popery, which increasing knowledge will bring into disuse.

They have opinions which cannot be ranked with superstition, because they regard only natural effects. They expect better crops of grain, by sowing their seed in the moon's increase. The moon has great influence in vulgar philosophy. In my memory it was a precept annually given in one of the *English* almanacs, *to kill hogs when the moon was increasing, and the bacon wold prove the better in boiling.*

We should have little claim to the praise of curiosity, if we had not endeavoured with particular attention to examine the question of the *Second Sight*. Of an opinion received for centuries by a whole nation, and supposed to be confirmed through its whole descent, by a series of successive facts, it is desirable that the truth should be established, or the fallacy detected.

The *Second Sight* is an impression made either by the mind upon the eye, or by the eye upon the mind, by which things distant or future are perceived, and seen as if they were present. A man on a journey far from home falls from his horse, another, who is perhaps at work about the house, sees him bleeding on the ground, commonly with a landscape of the place where the accident befalls him. Another seer, driving home his cattle, or wandering in idleness, or musing in the sunshine, is suddenly surprised by the appearance of a bridal ceremony, or funeral procession, and counts the mourners or attendants, of whom, if he knows them, he relates the names, if he knows them not, he can describe the dresses. Things distant are seen at the instant when they happen. Of things future I know not that there is any rule for determining the time between the Sight and the event.

This receptive faculty, for power it cannot be called, is neither voluntary nor constant. The appearances have no dependence upon choice; they cannot be summoned, detained, or recalled. The impression is sudden, and the effect often painful.

By the term *Second Sight*, seems to be meant a mode of seeing, superadded to that which Nature generally bestows. In the *Earse* it is called *Taisch*, which signifies likewise a spectre, or a vision. I know not, nor is it likely that the Highlanders ever examined, whether by *Taisch*, used for *Second Sight*, they mean the power of seeing or the thing seen.

I do not find it to be true, as it is reported, that to the *Second Sight* nothing is presented but phantoms of evil. Good seems to have the same proportion in these visionary scenes as it obtains in real life: almost all remarkable events have evil for their basis; and are either miseries incurred or miseries escaped. Our sense is so much stronger of what we suffer, than of what we enjoy, that the ideas of pain predominate in almost every mind. What is recollection but a revival of vexations, or history but a record of wars, treasons, and calamities? Death, which is considered as the greatest evil, happens to all. The greatest good, be it what it will, is the lot but of a part.

That they should often see death is to be expected; because death is an event frequent and important. But they see likewise more pleasing incidents. A gentleman told me, that when he had once gone far from his own Island, one of his labouring servants predicted his return, and described the livery of his attendant, which he had never worn at home; and which had been, without any previous design, occasionally given him.

Our desire for information was keen, and our inquiry frequent. Mr. Boswell's frankness and gaiety made everybody communicative; and we heard many tales of these airy shows, with more or less evidence and distinctness.

It is the common talk of the Lowland *Scots*, that the notion of the *Second Sight* is wearing away with other superstitions; and that its reality is no longer supposed but by the grossest people. How far its prevalence ever extended, or what ground is has lost, I know not. The Islanders of all degrees, whether of rank or understanding, universally admit it, except the ministers, who universally deny it, and are suspected to deny it, in consequence of a system, against conviction. One of them honestly told me, that he came to *Sky* with a resolution not to believe it.

Strong reasons for incredulity will readily occur. This faculty of seeing things out of sight is local, and commonly useless. It is a breach of the common order of things, without any visible reason or perceptible benefit. It is ascribed only to a people very little enlightened; and among them, for the most part, to the mean and the ignorant.

To the confidence of these objections it may be replied, that by presuming to determine what is fit, and what is beneficial, they presuppose more knowledge of the universal system than man has attained; and therefore depend upon principles too complicated and extensive for our comprehension; and that there can be no security in the consequence, when the premises are not understood; that the *Second Sight* is only wonderful because it is rare, for, considered in itself, it evolves no more difficulty than dreams, or perhaps than the regular exercise of the cogitative faculty; that a general opinion of communicative impulses, or visionary representations, has prevailed in all ages and all nations; that particular instances have been given, as neither *Bacon* nor *Bayle* has been able to resist; that sudden impressions, which the event has verified, have been felt by more than own or publish them; that the *Second Sight* of the *Hebrides* implies only the local frequency of a power, which is nowhere totally unknown; and that where we are unable to decide by antecedent reason, we must be content to yield to the force of testimony.

By pretension to *Second Sight*, no profit was ever sought or gained.

It is an involuntary affection, in which neither hope nor fear are known to have any part. Those who profess to feel it, do not boast of it as a privilege, nor are considered by others as advantageously distinguished. They have no temptation to feign; and their hearers have no motive to encourage the imposture.

To talk with any of these seers is not easy. There is one living in *Sky*, with whom we would have gladly conversed; but he is very gross and ignorant, and knew no *English*. The proportion in these countries of the poor to the rich is such, that if we suppose the quality to be accidental, it can very rarely happen to a man of education; and yet on such men it has sometimes fallen. There is now a Second Sighted gentleman in the Highlands, who complains of the terrors to which he is exposed.

The foresight of the Seers is not always prescience: they are impressed with images, of which the event only shows them the meaning. They tell what they have seen to others, who are at that time not more knowing than themselves, but may become at last very adequate witnesses, by comparing the narrative with its verification.

To collect sufficient testimonies for the satisfaction of the publick, or of ourselves, would have required more time than we could bestow. There is, against it, the seeming analogy of things confusedly seen, and little understood; and for it, the indistinct cry of national persuasion, which may be perhaps resolved at last into prejudice and tradition. I never could advance my curiosity to conviction; but came away at last only willing to believe.

As there subsists no longer in the Islands much of that peculiar and discriminative form of life, of which the idea had delighted our imagination, we were willing to listen to such accounts of past times as would be given us. But we soon found what memorials were to be expected from an illiterate people, whose whole time is a series of distress; where every morning is labouring with expedients for the evening; and where all mental pains or pleasure arose from the dread of winter, the expectation of spring, the caprices of their Chiefs, and the motions of the neighbouring Clans; where there was neither shame from ignorance, nor pride in knowledge; neither curiosity to inquire, nor vanity to communicate.

The *Chiefs* indeed were exempt from urgent penury, and daily difficulties; and in their houses were preserved what accounts remained of past ages. But the chiefs were sometimes ignorant and careless, and sometimes kept busy by turbulence and contention; and one generation of ignorance effaces the whole series of unwritten history. Books are faithful repositories, which may be awhile neglected or forgotten; but when they are opened again, will again impart their instruction: memory, once interrupted, is not to be recalled. Written learning is a fixed luminary, which, after the cloud that had hidden it has past away, is again bright in its proper station. Tradition is but a meteor, which, if once it falls, cannot be rekindled.

It seems to be universally supposed, that much of the local history was preserved by the Bards, of whom one is said to have been retained by every great family. After these Bards were some of my first inquiries; and I received such answers as, for awhile, made me please myself with my increase of knowledge; for I had not then learned how to estimate the narration of a Highlander.

They said that a great family had a *Bard* and a *Senachi*, who were the poet and historian of the house; and an old gentleman told me that he remembered one of each. Here was a dawn of intelligence. Of men that had lived within memory some certain knowledge might be attained. Though the office had ceased, its effects might continue; the poems might be found though there was no poet.

Another conversation indeed informed me, that the same man was both *Bard* and *Senachi*. This variation discouraged me; but as the practice might be different in different times, or at the same time in different families, there was yet no reason for supposing that I must necessarily sit down in total ignorance.

Soon after I was told by a gentleman who is generally acknowledged the greatest master of *Hebridian* antiquities, that there had indeed once been both Bards and Senachies; and that *Senachi* signified *the man of talk*, or of conversation; but that neither Bard nor Senachi had existed for some centuries. I have no reason to suppose it exactly known at what time the custom ceased, nor did it probably cease in all houses at once. But whenever the practice of recitation was disused, the works, whether poetical or historical, perished with the authors; for in those times nothing had been written in the *Earse* language.

Whether the *Man of talk* was a historian, whose office was to tell truth, or a story-teller like those which were in the last century, and perhaps are now among the Irish, whose trade was only to amuse, it would now be in vain to inquire.

Most of the domestick offices were, I believe, hereditary; and probably the laureat of a Clan was always the son of the last laureat. The history of the race could no otherwise be communicated or retained; but what genius could be expected in a poet by inheritance?

The nation was wholly illiterate. Neither Bards nor Senachies could write or read; but if they were ignorant, there was no danger of detection; they were believed by those whose vanity they flattered.

The recital of genealogies, which has been considered as very efficacious to the preservation of a true series of ancestry, was anciently made, when the heir of the family came to manly age. This practice has never subsisted within time of memory, nor was much credit due to such rehearsers, who might obtrude fictitious pedigrees, either to please their masters, or to hide the deficiency of their own memories.

Where the Chiefs of the Highlands have found the histories of their descent it is difficult to tell; for no *Earse* genealogy was ever written. In general this only is evident, that the principal house of a clan must be very ancient, and that those must have lived long in a place, of whom it is not known when they came thither.

Thus hopeless are all attempts to find any traces of Highland learning. Nor are their primitive customs and ancient manner of life otherwise than very faintly and uncertainly remembered by the present race.

The peculiarities which strike the native of a commercial country, proceeded in a great measure from the want of money. To the servants and dependants that were not domesticks, and if an estimate be made from the capacity of any of their old houses which I have seen, their domesticks could have been but few, were appropriated certain portions of land for their support. *Macdonald* has a piece of ground yet, called the Bards or Senachies field. When a beef was killed for the house, particular parts were claimed as fees by the several officers, or workmen. What was the right of each I have not learned. The head belonged to the smith, and the udder of a cow to the piper; the weaver had likewise his particular part; and so many pieces followed these prescriptive claims, that the Laird's was at last but little.

The payment of rent in kind has been so long disused in England, that it is totally forgotten. It was practised very lately in the *Hebrides*, and probably still continues, not only in St. *Kilda*, where money is not yet known, but in others of the smaller and remoter Islands. It were perhaps to be desired, that no change in this particular should have been made. When the Laird could only eat the produce of his lands, he was under the necessity of residing upon them; and when the tenant could not convert his stock into more portable riches, he could never be tempted away from his farm, from the only place where he could be wealthy. Money confounds subordination, by overpowering the distinctions of rank and birth, and weakens authority by supplying power of resistance, or expedients for escape. The feudal system is formed for a nation employed in agriculture, and has never long kept its hold where gold and silver have become common.

The arms were anciently the *Glaymore*, or great two-handed sword, and afterwards the two-edged sword and target, or buckler, which was sustained on the left arm. In the midst of the target, which was made of wood, covered with leather, and studded with nails, a slender lance, about two feet long, was sometimes fixed; it was heavy and cumberous, and accordingly has for some time past been gradually laid aside. Very few targets were at Culloden. The dirk or broad dagger, I am afraid, was of more use in private quarrels than in battles. The Lochaber-ax is only a slight alteration of the old *English* bill.

After all that has been said of the force and terrour of the Highland sword, I could not find that the art of defence was any part of common education. The gentlemen were perhaps sometimes skilful gladiators, but the common men had no other powers than those of violence and courage. Yet it is well known, that the onset of the Highlanders was very formidable. As an army cannot consist of philosophers, a panick is easily excited by any unwonted mode of annoyance. New dangers are naturally magnified; and men accustomed only to exchange bullets at a distance, and rather to hear their enemies than see them, are discouraged and amazed when they find themselves encountered hand to hand, and catch the gleam of steel flashing in their faces.

The Highland weapons gave opportunity for many exertions of personal courage, and sometimes for single combats in the field, like those which occur so frequently in fabulous wars. At Falkirk, a gentleman now living, was, I suppose after the retreat of the King's troops, engaged at a distance from the rest with an Irish dragoon. They were both skilful swordsmen, and the contest was not easily decided; the dragoon at last had the advantage, and the Highlander called for quarter; but quarter was refused him, and the fight continued till he was reduced to defend himself upon his knee. At that instant one of the Macleods came to his rescue; who, as it is said, offered quarter to the dragoon, but he thought himself obliged to reject what he had before refused, and, as battle gives little time to deliberate, was immediately killed.

Funerals were formerly solemnized by calling multitudes together, and entertaining them at great expense. This emulation of useless cost has been for some time discouraged, and at last, in the Isle of *Sky*, is almost suppressed.

Of the Earse language, as I understand nothing, I cannot say more than I have been told. It is the rude speech of a barbarous people, who had few thoughts to express, and were content, as they conceived grossly, to be grossly understood. After what has been lately talked of Highland Bards, and Highland genius, many will startle when they are told, that the *Earse* never was a written language; that there is not in the world an Earse manuscript a hundred years old; and that the sounds of the Highlanders were never expressed by letters, till some little books of piety were translated, and a metrical version of the Psalms was made by the Synod of *Argyle*. Whoever therefore now writes in this language, spells according to his own perception of the sound, and his own idea of the power of the letters. The *Welsh* and the *Irish* are cultivated tongues. The Welsh, two hundred years ago, insulted their *English* neighbours for the instability of their Orthography; while the *Earse* merely floated in the breath of the people, and could therefore receive little improvement.

When a language begins to teem with books, it is tending to

refinement; as those who undertake to teach others must have undergone some labour in improving themselves, they set a proportionate value on their own thoughts, and wish to enforce them by efficacious expressions; speech becomes embodied and permanent; different modes and phrases are compared, and the best obtains an establishment. By degrees one age improves upon another. Exactness is first obtained, and afterwards elegance. But diction, merely vocal, is always in its childhood. As no man leaves his eloquence behind him, the new generations have all to learn. There may possibly be books without a polished language, but there can be no polished language without books.

That the Bards could not read more than the rest of their countrymen, it is reasonable to suppose; because, if they had read, they could probably have written; and how high their compositions may reasonably be rated, an inquirer may best judge by considering what stores of imagery, what principles of ratiocination, what comprehension of knowledge, and what delicacy of elocution, he has known any man attain who cannot read. The state of the Bards was yet more hopeless. He that cannot read, may now converse with those that can; but the Bard was a barbarian among barbarians, who, knowing nothing himself, lived with others that knew no more.

There has lately been in the Islands one of these illiterate poets, who hearing the Bible read at church, is said to have turned the sacred history into verse. I heard part of a dialogue, composed by him, translated by a young lady in *Mull*, and thought it had more meaning that I expected from a man totally uneducated; but he had some opportunities of knowledge; he lived among a learned people. After all that has been done for the instruction of the Highlanders, the antipathy between their language and literature still continues; and no man that has learned only *Earse* is, at this time, able to read.

The *Earse* has many dialects, and the words used in some Islands are not always known in others. In literate nations, though the pronunciation, and sometimes the words of common speech may differ, as now in *England*, compared with the south of *Scotland*, yet there is a written diction, which pervades all dialects, and is understood in every province. But where the whole language is colloquial, he that has only one part, never gets the rest, as he cannot get it but by change of residence.

In an unwritten speech, nothing that is not very short is transmitted from one generation to another. Few have opportunities of hearing a long composition often enough to learn it, or have inclination to repeat it so often as is necessary to retain it; and what is once forgotten is lost for ever. I believe there cannot be recovered, in the whole *Earse* language, five hundred lines of which there is any evidence to prove them a hundred years old. Yet I hear that the father of Ossian boasts of two chests more of ancient poetry, which he suppresses, because they are too good for the *English*.

He that goes into the Highlands with a mind naturally acquiescent, and a credulity eager for wonders, may come back with an opinion very different from mine; for the inhabitants, knowing the ignorance of all strangers in their language and antiquities, perhaps are not very scrupulous adherents to the truth; yet I do not say that they deliberately speak studied falsehood, or have a settled purpose to deceive. They have inquired and considered little, and do not always feel their own ignorance. They are not much accustomed to be interrogated by others, and seem never to have thought upon interrogating themselves; so that if they do not know what they tell to be true, they likewise do not distinctly perceive it to be false.

Mr. Boswell was very diligent in his inquiries; and the result of his investigations was, that the answer to the second question was commonly such as nullified the answer to the first.

We were awhile told, that they had an old translation of the scriptures; and told it till it would appear obstinacy to inquire again. Yet by continued accumulation of questions we found, that the translation meant, if any meaning there were, was nothing less than the *Irish* Bible.

We heard of manuscripts that were, or that had been in the hands of somebody's father, or grandfather; but at last we had no reason to believe that they were other than Irish. Martin mentions Irish, but never any Earse manuscripts to be found in the Islands of his time.

I suppose my opinion of the poems of Ossian is already discovered. I believe they never existed in any other form than that which we have seen. The editor, or author, never could shew the original; nor can it be shewn by any other; to revenge reasonable incredulity, by refusing evidence, is a degree of insolence, with which the world is not yet acquainted; and stubborn audacity is the last refuge of guilt. It would be easy to shew it if he had it; but whence could it be had? It is too long to be remembered, and the language formerly had nothing written. He has doubtless inserted names that circulate in popular stories, and may have translated some wandering ballads, if any can be found; and the names and some of the images being recollected, make an inaccurate auditor imagine, by the help of Caledonian bigotry, that he has formerly heard the whole.

I asked a very learned Minister in *Sky*, who had used all arts to make me believe the genuineness of the book, whether at last he believed it himself? but he would not answer. He wished me to be deceived for the honour of his country; but would not directly and formally deceive me. Yet has this man's testimony been publickly produced, as of one that held Fingal to be the work of Ossian.

It is said, that some men of integrity profess to have heard parts of it, but they all heard them when they were boys; and it never was said that any of them could recite six lines. They remember names, and perhaps some proverbial sentiments; and having no distinct ideas, coin a resemblance without an original. The persuasion of the Scots, however, is far from universal; and in a question so capable of proof, why should doubt be suffered to continue? The editor has been heard to say, that part of the poem was received by him in the Saxon character. He has then found, by some peculiar fortune, an unwritten language, written in a character which the natives probably never beheld.

I have yet supposed no imposture but in the publisher; yet I am far from certainty, that some translations have not been lately made, that may now be obtruded as parts of the original work. Credulity on one part is a strong temptation to deceit on the other, especially to deceit of which no personal injury is the consequence, and which flatters the author with his own ingenuity. The Scots have something to plead for their easy reception of an improbable fiction: they are seduced by their fondness for their supposed ancestors. A Scotchman must be a very sturdy moralist, who does not love *Scotland* better than truth; he will always love it better than inquiry: and if falsehood flatters his vanity, will not be very diligent to detect it. Neither ought the *English* to be much influenced by *Scotch* authority; for of the past and present state of the whole *Earse* nation the Lowlanders are at least as ignorant as ourselves. To be ignorant is painful; but it is dangerous to quiet our uneasiness by the delusive opiate of hasty persuasion.

But this is the age in which those who could not read, have been supposed to write; in which the giants of antiquated romance have been exhibited as realities. If we know little of the ancient Highlanders, let us not fill the vacuity with *Ossian*. If we have not searched the *Magellanick* regions, let us, however, forbear to people them with *Patagons*.

Having waited some days at *Armidel*, we were flattered at last with a wind that promised to convey us to *Mull*. We went on board a boat that was taking in kelp, and left the Isle of *Sky* behind us. We were doomed to experience, like others, the danger of trusting to the wind, which blew against us, in a short time, with such violence, that we, being no seasoned sailors, were willing to call it a tempest. I was sea-sick and lay down. Mr. *Boswell* kept the deck. The master knew not well whither to go; and our difficulties might perhaps have filled a very pathetick page, had not Mr. *Maclean* of *Col*, who with every other qualification which insular life requires, is a very active and skilful mariner, piloted us safe into his own harbour.

COL

In the morning we found ourselves under the Isle of *Col*, where we landed, and passed the first day and night with Captain *Maclean*, a gentleman who has lived for some time in the East Indies; but having dethroned no Nabob, is not too rich to settle in his own country.

Next day the wind was fair, and we might have had an easy passage to *Mull*; but having, contrarily to our own intention, landed upon a new Island, we would not leave it wholly unexamined. We therefore suffered the vessel to depart without us, and trusted the skies for another wind.

Mr. *Maclean of Col*, having a very numerous family, has, for some time past, resided at *Aberdeen*, that he may superintend their education, and leaves the young gentleman, our friend, to govern his dominions, with the full power of a Highland Chief. By the absence of the Laird's family, our entertainment was made more difficult, because the house was in a great degree disfurnished; but young Col's kindness and activity supplied all defects, and procured us more than sufficient accommodation.

Here I first mounted a little Highland steed; and, if there had been many spectators, should have been somewhat ashamed of my figure in the march. The horses of the Islands, as of other barren countries, are very low: they are indeed musculous and strong, beyond what their size gives reason for expecting; but a bulky man upon one of their backs makes a very disproportionate appearance.

From the habitation of Captain *Maclean* we went to *Grissipol*, but called by the way on Mr. *Hector Maclean*, the minister of Col, whom we found in a hut, that is, a house of only one floor, but with windows and chimney, and not inelegantly furnished. Mr. *Maclean* has the reputation of great learning; he is seventy-seven years old,

The island of Coll where Johnson was so happily storm bound is one of the most unspoilt of the Hebridean islands. It has a population of 150, and public services are such that one would be unlikely to be stranded for long nowadays!

but not infirm, with a look of venerable dignity, excelling what I remember in any other man.

His conversation was not unsuitable to his appearance. I lost some of his good-will, by treating a heretical writer with more regard than, in his opinion, a heretick could deserve. I honoured his orthodoxy, and did not much censure his asperity. A man who has settled his opinions, does not love to have the tranquillity of his conviction disturbed; and at seventy-seven it is time to be in earnest.

Mention was made of the *Earse* translation of the New Testament, which has been lately published, and of which the learned Mr. *Macqueen* of *Sky* spoke with commendation; but Mr. *Maclean* said he did not use it, because he could make the text more intelligible to his auditors by an extemporary version. From this I inferred, that the language of the translation was not the language of the Isle of *Col*.

He has no publick edifice for the exercise of his ministry; and can officiate to no greater number than a room can contain; and the room of a hut is not very large. This is all the opportunity of worship that is now granted to the inhabitants of the Island, some of whom must travel thither perhaps ten miles. Two chapels were erected by their ancestors, of which I saw the skeletons, which now stand faithful witnesses of the triumph of Reformation.

The want of churches is not the only impediment to piety: there is likewise a want of Ministers. A parish often contains more Islands than one, and each island can have the Minister only in its turn. At *Raasa* they had, I think, a right to service only every third Sunday. All the provision made by the present ecclesiastical constitution, for the inhabitants of about a hundred square miles, is a prayer and a sermon in a little room, once in three weeks: and even this parsimonious distribution is at the mercy of the weather: and in those Islands where the minister does not reside, it is impossible to tell how many weeks or months may pass without any publick exercise of religion.

GRISSIPOL IN COL

After a short conversation with Mr. *Maclean*, we went on to *Grissipol*, a house and farm tenanted by Mr. *Macsweyn*, where I saw more of the ancient life of a Highlander than I had yet found. Mrs. *Macsweyn* could speak no *English*, and had never seen any other places than the Islands of *Sky*, *Mull*, and *Col*: but she was hospitable and good-humoured, and spread her table with sufficient liberality. We found tea here, as in every other place, but our spoons were of horn.

The house of *Grissipol* stands by a brook very clear and quick; which is, I suppose, one of the most copious streams in the Island. This place was the scene of an action, much celebrated in the traditional history of Col, but which probably no two relaters will tell alike.

Some time, in the obscure ages, *Macneil* of *Barra* married the Lady *Maclean*, who had the Isle of Col for her jointure. Whether *Macneil* detained *Col*, when the widow was dead, or whether she lived so long as to make her heirs impatient, is perhaps not now known. The younger son, called *John Gerves*, or *John the Giant*, a man of great strength, who was then in *Ireland*, either for safety, or for education, dreamed of recovering his inheritance; and getting some adventurers together, which in those unsettled times was not hard to do, invaded Col. He was driven away, but was not discouraged, and collecting new followers, in three years came again with fifty men. In his way he stopped at *Artorinish* in *Morvern*, where his uncle was prisoner to *Macleod*, and was then with his enemies in a tent. *Maclean* took with him only one servant, whom he ordered to stay at the outside; and where he should see the tent pressed outwards, to strike with his dirk; it being the intention of *Maclean*, as any man provoked him, to lay hands upon him, and push him back. He entered the tent alone, with his *Lochabar-ax* in his hand, and struck such terror into the whole assembly, that they dismissed his uncle.

When he landed at Col, he saw the sentinel, who kept watch towards the sea, running off to *Grissipol*, to give *Macneil*, who was there with a hundred and twenty men, an account of the invasion. He told *Macgill*, one of his followers, that if he intercepted that dangerous intelligence, by catching the courier, he would give him certain lands in *Mull*. Upon this promise, *Macgill* pursued the messenger, and either killed, or stopped him; and his posterity, till very lately, held the lands in *Mull*.

The alarm being thus prevented, he came unexpectedly upon *Macneil*. Chiefs were in those days never wholly unprovided for an enemy. A fight ensued, in which one of their followers is said to have given an extraordinary proof of activity, by bounding backwards over the brook of *Grissipol*. *Macneil* being killed, and many of his clan destroyed, *Maclean* took possession of the Island, which the *Macneils* attempted to conquer by another invasion, but were defeated and repulsed.

Maclean, in his turn, invaded the estate of the *Macneils*, took the castle of *Brecacig*, and conquered the Isle of *Barra*, which he held for seven years, and then restored it to the heirs.

CASTLE OF COL

From *Grissipol*, Mr. *Maclean* conducted us to his father's seat; a neat new house, erected near the old castle, I think, by the last proprietor. Here we were allowed to take our station, and lived very commodiously, while we waited for moderate weather and a fair wind, which we did not so soon obtain, but we had time to get some information of the present state of *Col*, partly by inquiry, and partly by occasional excursions.

Col is computed to be thirteen miles in length, and three in breadth. Both the ends are the property of the Duke of *Argyle*, but the middle belongs to *Maclean*, who is called *Col*, as the only Laird.

Col, is not properly rocky; it is rather one continued rock, of a surface much diversified with protuberances, and covered with a thin layer of earth, which is often broken, and discovers the stone. Such a soil is not for plants that strike deep roots; and perhaps in the whole Island nothing has ever yet grown to the height of a table. The uncultivated parts are clothed with heath, among which industry has interspersed spots of grass and corn; but no attempt has yet been made to raise a tree. Young *Col*, who has a very laudable desire of improving his patrimony, purposes some time to plant an orchard; which, if it be sheltered by a wall, may perhaps succeed. He has introduced the culture of turnips, of which he has a field, where the whole work was performed by his own hand. His intention is to provide food for his cattle in the winter. This innovation was considered by Mr. *Macsweyn* as the idle project of a young head heated with *English* fancies; but he has now found that turnips will really grow, and that hungry sheep and cows will really eat them.

By such acquisitions as these the Hebrides may in time rise above their annual distress. Wherever heath will grow, there is reason to think something better may draw nourishment; and by trying the production of other places, plants will be found suitable to every soil.

Col has many lochs, some of which have trouts and eels, and others have never yet been stocked; another proof of the negligence of the Islanders, who might take fish in the inland waters when they cannot go to sea.

Their quadrupeds are horses, cows, sheep, and goats. They have neither deer, hares, nor rabbits. They have no vermin, except rats, which have been lately brought thither by sea, as to other places; and are free from serpents, frogs, and toads.

The harvest in *Col* and in *Lewis*, is ripe sooner than in *Sky*, and the winter in *Col* is never cold, but very tempestuous. I know not that I ever heard the wind so loud in any other place; and Mr. *Boswell* observed, that its noise was all its own, for there were no trees to increase it.

Noise is not the worst effect of the tempests; for they have thrown the sand from the shore over a considerable part of the land; and it is said still to encroach and destroy more and more pasture; but I am not of opinion, that by any surveys or landmarks, its limits have been ever fixed, or its progression ascertained. If one man has confidence enough to say, that it advances, nobody can bring any proof to support him in denying it. The reason why it is not spread

The Laird's House on Coll, drawn by Lancelot Speed for George Birbeck Hill in 1889. The old castle has now been beautifully restored, and the new castle is being converted into flats.

to a greater extent, seems to be that the wind and rain come almost together, and that it is made close and heavy by the wet before the storms can put it in motion. So thick is the bed, and so small the particles, that if a traveller should be caught by a sudden gust in dry weather, he would find it very difficult to escape with life.

For natural curiosities, I was shown only two great masses of stone, which lie loose upon the ground; one on the top of a hill and the other at a small distance from the bottom. They certainly were never put into their present places by human strength or skill; and though an earthquake might have broken off the lower stone, and rolled it into the valley, no account can be given of the other, which lies on the hill, unless, which I forgot to examine, there be still near it some higher rock, from which it might be torn. All nations have a tradition, that their earliest ancestors were giants, and these stones are said to have been thrown up and down by a giant and his mistress. There are so many more important things, of which human knowledge can give no account, that it may be forgiven us if we speculate no longer on two stones in Col.

This Island is very populous. About nine-and-twenty years ago, the fencible men of *Col* were reckoned one hundred and forty, which is the sixth of eight hundred and forty; and probably some contrived to be left out of the list. The Minister told us, that a few years ago the inhabitants were eight hundred, between the ages of seven and seventy. Round numbers are seldom exact. But in this case the authority is good, and the error likely to be little. If to the eight hundred be added what the laws of computation require, they will be increased to at least a thousand; and if the dimensions of the country have been accurately related, every mile maintains more than twenty-five.

This proportion of habitation is greater than the appearance of the country seems to admit; for wherever the eye wanders, it sees much waste and little cultivation. I am more inclined to extend the land, of which no measure has ever been taken, than to diminish the people, who have been really numbered. Let it be supposed, that a computed mile contains a mile and a half, as was commonly found true in the mensuration of the *English* roads, and we shall then allot nearly twelve to a mile, which agrees much better with ocular observation.

Here, as in *Sky* and other Islands, are the Laird, the Tacksmen, and the under-tenants.

Mr. *Maclean*, the laird, has very extensive possessions, being proprietor, not only of far the greater part of *Col*, but of the extensive island of *Rum*, and a very considerable territory in *Mull*.

Rum is one of the larger Islands, almost square, and therefore of great capacity in proportion to its sides. By the usual method of estimating computed extent, it may contain more than a hundred and twenty square miles.

It originally belonged to *Clanronald*, and was purchased by *Col*, who, in some dispute about the bargain, made *Clanronald* prisoner, and kept him nine months in confinement. Its owner represents it as mountainous, rugged, and barren. In the hills there are red deer. The horses are very small, but a breed eminent for beauty. *Col*, not long ago, bought one of them from a tenant; who told him, that as he was of a shape uncommonly elegant, he could not sell him but at a high price; and that whoever had him should pay a guinea and a half.

There are said to be in *Barra*, a race of horses yet smaller, of which the highest is not above thirty-six inches.

The rent of *Rum* is not great. Mr. Maclean declared, that he should be very rich, if he could set his land at twopence halfpenny an acre. The inhabitants are fifty eight families, who continued Papists for some time after the Laird became a Protestant. Their adherence to their old religion was strengthened by the countenance of the Laird's sister, a zealous Romanist, till one Sunday, as they were going to mass under the conduct of their patroness, *Maclean* met them on the way, gave one of them a blow on the head with a *yellow stick*, I suppose a cane, for which the *Earse* had no name, and drove them to the kirk, from which they have never since departed. Since the use of this method of conversion, the inhabitants of *Egg* and *Canna*, who continue Papists, call the Protestantism of *Rum*, the religion of the *Yellow Stick*.

The only Popish Islands are *Egg* and *Canna*. *Egg*, is the principal Island of a parish, in which, though he has no congregation, the Protestant Minister resides. I have heard of nothing curious in it, but the cave in which a former generation of the Islanders were smothered by *Macleod*.

If we had travelled with more leisure, it had not been fit to have neglected the Popish Islands. Popery is favourable to ceremony; and among ignorant nations, ceremony is the only preservative of tradition. Since protestantism was extended to the savage parts of Scotland, it has perhaps been one of the chief labours of the Ministers to abolish stated observances, because they continued the remembrance of the former religion. We therefore who came to hear old traditions, and see antiquated manners, should probably have found them amongst the Papists.

Canna, the other Popish Island, belongs to *Clanronald*. It is said not to comprise more than twelve miles of land, and yet maintains as many inhabitants as *Rum*.

We were at *Col* under the protection of the young Laird, without any of the distresses, which Mr. *Pennant*, in a fit of simple credulity, seems to think almost worthy of an elegy by Ossian. Wherever we roved, we were pleased to see the reverence with which his subjects regarded him. He did not endeavour to dazzle them by any magnificence of dress; his only distinction was a feather in his bonnet; but as soon as he appeared, they forsook their work, and clustered about him: he took them by the hand, and they seemed mutually delighted. He has the proper disposition of a Chieftain, and seems desirous to continue the customs of his house. The bagpiper played regularly, when dinner was served, whose person and dress made a good appearance; and he brought no disgrace upon the family of *Rankin*, which has long supplied the lairds of *Col* with hereditary musick.

The tacksmen of *Col* seem to live with less dignity and convenience than those of *Sky*; where they have good houses, and tables not only plentiful but delicate. In *Col* only two houses pay the window-tax; for only two have six windows, which, I suppose, are the Laird's and Mr. *Macsweyn's*.

The rents have, till within seven years, been paid in kind, but the tenants finding that cattle and corn varied in their price, desired for the future to give their landlord money; which, not having yet arrived at the philosophy of commerce, they consider as being every year of the same value.

We were told of a particular mode of undertenure. The Tacksman admits some of his inferior neighbours to the cultivation of his grounds, on condition that performing all the work, and giving a third part of the seed, they shall keep a certain number of cows, sheep, and goats, and reap a third part of the harvest. Thus, by less than the tillage of two acres, they pay the rent of one.

There are tenants below the rank of Tacksmen, that have got smaller tenants under them; for in every place, where money is not the general equivalent, there must be some whose labour is immediately paid by daily food.

A country that has no money, is by no means convenient for beggars, both because such countries are commonly poor, and because charity requires some trouble and some thought. A penny is easily given upon the first impulse of compassion, or impatience of importunity; but few will deliberately search their cupboards or their granaries to find out something to give. A penny is likewise easily spent; but victuals, if they are unprepared, require houseroom, and fire, and utensils, which the beggar knows not where to find.

Yet beggars there sometimes are, who wander from Island to Island. We had, in our passage to *Mull*, the company of a woman and her child, who had exhausted the charity of *Col*. The arrival of a beggar on an Island is accounted a sinistrous event. Every body considers that he shall have the less for what he gives away. Their alms, I believe, is generally oatmeal.

Near to Col is another island called *Tireye*, eminent for its fertility. Though it has but half the extent of *Rum*, it is so well peopled that there have appeared, not long ago, nine hundred and fourteen at a funeral. The plenty of this island enticed beggars to it, who seemed so burdensome to the inhabitants, that a formal compact was drawn up, by which they obliged themselves to grant no more relief to casual wanderers, because they had among them an indigent woman of high birth, whom they considered as entitled to all that they could spare. I have read the stipulation, which was indited with juridical formality, but was never made valid by regular subscription.

If the inhabitants of *Col* have nothing to give, it is not that they are oppressed by their landlord; their leases seem to be very profitable. One farmer, who pays only seven pounds a year, has maintained seven daughters and three sons, of whom the eldest is educated at *Aberdeen* for the ministry; and now, at every vacation, opens a school in *Col*.

Life is here, in some respects, improved beyond the condition of some other Islands. In *Sky* what is wanted can only be bought as the arrival of some wandering pedlar may afford an opportunity; but in *Col* there is a standing shop, and in *Mull* there are two. A shop in the Islands, as in other places of little frequentation, is a repository of everything requisite for common use. Mr. *Boswell's* journal was filled, and he brought some paper in *Col*. To a man that ranges the streets of *London*, where he is tempted to contrive wants for the pleasure of supplying them, a shop affords no image worthy of attention; but in an Island, it turns the balance of existence between good and evil. To live in perpetual want of little things, is a state not indeed of torture, but of constant vexation. I have in *Sky* had some difficulty to find ink for a letter; and if a woman breaks her needle, her work is at a stop.

As it is, the Islanders are obliged to content themselves with succedaneous means for many common purposes. I have seen the chief man of a very wide district riding with a halter for a bridle, and governing his hobby with a wooden curb.

The people of *Col*, however, do not want dexterity to supply some of their necessities. Several arts which make trades, and demand apprenticeships in great cities, are here the practices of daily economy. In every house candles are made, both moulded and dipped. Their wicks are small shreds of linen cloth. They all know how to extract from the Cuddy, oil for their lamps. They all tan skins, and make brogues.

As we travelled through *Sky*, we saw many cottages, but they very frequently stood single on the naked ground. In *Col*, where the hills opened a place convenient for habitation, we found a petty village, of which every hut had a little garden adjoining; thus they made an appearance of social commerce and mutual offices, and of some attention to convenience and future supply. There is not in the *Western Islands* any collection of buildings that can make pretensions to be called a town, except in the *Isle of Lewis*, which I have not seen.

If *Lewis* is distinguished by a town, *Col* has also something peculiar. The young Laird has attempted what perhaps no islander ever thought on. He has begun a road capable of a wheel-carriage. He has carried it about a mile, and will continue it by annual elongation from his house to the harbour.

Of taxes, here is no reason for complaining; they are paid by a very easy composition. The *malt-tax* for *Col* is twenty shillings. Whisky is very plentiful: there are several stills in the Island, and more is made than the inhabitants consume.

The great business of insular policy is now to keep the people in their own country. As the world has been let in upon them, they have heard of happier climates, and less arbitrary government; and if they are disgusted, have emissaries among them ready to offer them land and houses, as a reward for deserting their Chief and Clan. Many have departed both from the main of *Scotland*, and from the Islands; and all that go may be considered as subjects lost to the *British* crown; for a nation scattered in the boundless regions of *America* resembles rays diverging from a focus. All the rays remain, but the heat is gone. Their power consisted in their concentration: when they are dispersed, they have no effect.

It may be thought that they are happier by the change; but they are not happy as a nation, for they are a nation no longer. As they contribute not to the prosperity of any community, they must want that security, that dignity, that happiness, whatever it be, which a prosperous community throws back upon individuals.

The inhabitants of *Col* have not yet learned to be weary of their heath and rocks, but attend their agriculture and their dairies, without listening to American seducements.

There are some however who think that this emigration has raised terrour disproportionate to its real evil; and that it is only a new mode of doing what was always done. The Highlands, they say, never maintained their natural inhabitants; but the people, when they found themselves too numerous, instead of extending cultivation, provided for themselves by a more compendious method, and sought better fortune in other countries. They did not indeed go away in collective bodies, but withdrew invisibly, a few at a time; but the whole number of fugitives was not less, and the difference between other times and this, is only the same as between evaporation and effusion.

This is plausible, but I am afraid it is not true. Those who went before, if they were not sensibly missed, as the argument supposes, must have gone either in less number, or in a manner less detrimental, than at present; because formerly there was no complaint. Those who then left the country were generally the idle dependants on overburdened families, or men who had no property, and therefore carried away only themselves. In the present eagerness of emigration, families, and almost communities, go away together. Those who were considered as prosperous and wealthy, sell their stock, and carry away the money. Once none went away but the useless and poor; in some parts there is now reason to fear, that none will stay but those who are too poor to remove themselves, and too useless to be removed at the cost of others.

Of antiquity there is no more knowledge in *Col* than in other places; but everywhere something may be gleaned.

How ladies were portioned, when there was no money, it would be difficult for an *Englishman* to guess. In 1649, *Maclean* of *Duart* in *Mull* married his sister, *Fingala*, to *Maclean* of *Col*, with a hundred and eighty kine; and stipulated, that if she became a widow, her jointure should be three hundred and sixty. I suppose some proportionate tract of land was appropriated to their pasturage.

The disposition to pompous and expensive funerals, which has at one time or other prevailed in most parts of the civilised world, is not yet suppressed in the Islands, though some of the ancient solemnities are worn away, and singers are no longer hired to attend the procession. Nineteen years ago, at the burial of the laird of *Col*, were killed thirty cows, and about fifty sheep. The number of cows is positively told, and we must suppose other victuals in like proportion.

Mr. *Maclean* informed us of an odd game, of which he did not tell the original, but which may perhaps be used in other places, where the reason of it is not yet forgot. At New-year's eve, in the hall or castle of the Laird, where, at festal seasons, there may be supposed a very numerous company, one man dresses himself in a cow's hide, upon which other men beat with sticks. He runs with all this noise round the house, which all the company quits in a counterfeited fright: the door is then shut. At New-year's eve there is no great pleasure to be had out of doors in the *Hebrides*. They are sure soon to recover from their terrour to solicit for re-admission; which, for the honour of poetry, is not to be obtained but by repeating a verse, with which those that are knowing and provident take care to be furnished.

Very near the house of *Maclean* stands the castle of *Col*, which was the mansion of the Laird till the house was built. It is built upon a rock, as Mr. *Boswell* remarked, that it might not be mined. It is very strong, and having been not long uninhabited, is yet in repair. On the wall was, not long ago, a stone with an inscription, importing that *if any man of the clan of Maclonich shall appear before this castle, though he come at midnight, with a man's head in his hand, he shall there find safety and protection against all but the King.*

This is an old Highland treaty made upon a very memorable occasion. *Maclean*, the son of *John Gerves*, who recovered *Col*, and conquered *Barra*, had obtained, it is said, from *James* the Second, a grant of the lands of Lochiel, forfeited, I suppose, for some offence against the State.

Forfeited estates were not, in those days, quietly resigned; *Maclean*, therefore, went with an armed force to seize his new possessions, and I know not for what reason, took his wife with him. The *Camerons* rose in defence of their Chief, and a battle was fought at the head of *Loch Ness*, near the place where *Fort Augustus* now stands, in which *Lochiel* obtained the victory, and *Maclean*, with his followers, was defeated and destroyed.

The lady fell into the hands of the conquerors, and, being found pregnant, was placed in the custody of *Maclonich*, one of a tribe or family branched from *Cameron*, with orders, if she brought a boy, to destroy him, if a girl, to spare her.

Maclonich's wife, who was with child likewise, had a girl about the same time at which lady *Maclean* brought a boy, and *Maclonich* with more generosity to his captive, than fidelity to his trust, contrived that the children should be changed.

Maclean, being thus preserved from death, in time recovered his original patrimony; and in gratitude to his friend, made his castle a place of refuge to any of the Clan that should think himself in danger; and as a proof of the reciprocal confidence, *Maclean* took upon himself and his posterity, the care of educating the heir of *Maclonich*.

The story, like all other traditions of the Highlands, is variously related; but though some circumstances are uncertain, the principal fact is true. *Maclean* undoubtedly owed his preservation to *Maclonich*; for the treaty between the two families has been strictly observed: it did not sink into disuse or oblivion, but continued in its full force while the chieftains retained their power. I have read a demand of protection, made not more than thirty-seven years ago, for one of the *Maclonichs*, named *Ewen Cameron*, who had been accessory to the death of *Macmartin*, and had been banished by *Lochiel*, his lord, for a certain term; at the expiration of which he returned married from *France*, but the *Macmartins*, not satisfied with the punishment, when he attempted to settle, still threatened him with vengeance. He therefore asked, and obtained, shelter in the Isle of *Col*.

The power of protection subsists no longer; but what the law permits is yet continued, and *Maclean of Col* now educates the heir of *Maclonich*.

There still remains in the Islands, though it is passing fast away, the custom of fosterage. A Laird, a man of wealth and eminence, sends his child, either male of female, to a tacksman, or tenant, to be fostered. It is not always his own tenant, but some distant friend that obtains this honour; for an honour such a trust is very reasonably thought. The terms of fosterage seem to vary in different islands. In *Mull* the father sends with his child a certain number of cows, to which the same number is added by the fosterer. The father appropriates a proportionable extent of ground, without rent, for their pasturage. If every cow brings a calf, half belongs to the fosterer, and half to the child; but if there be only one calf between two cows, it is the child's, and when the child returns to the parents, it is accompanied by all the cows given, both by the father and by the fosterer, with half of the increase of the stock by propagation. These beasts are considered as a portion, and are called *Macalive* cattle, of which the father has the produce, but is supposed not to have the full property, but to owe the same number to the child, as a portion to the daughter, or stock for the son.

Children continued with the fosterer perhaps six years, and cannot, where this is the practice, be considered burdensome. The fosterer, if he gives four cows, receives likewise four, and has, while the child continues with him, grass for eight without rent, with half the calves, and all the milk, for which he pays only four cows when he dismisses his *Dalt*, for that is the name for a foster child.

Fosterage is, I believe, sometimes performed upon more liberal terms. Our friend, the young laird of *Col*, was fostered by *Macsweyn* of *Grissipol. Macsweyn* then lived a tenant to Sir *James Macdonald* in the Isle of *Sky*; and therefore *Col*, whether he sent him cattle or not, could grant him no land. The *Dalt*, however, at his return, brought back a considerable amount of *Macalive cattle*, and of the friendship so formed there have been good effects. When *Macdonald* raised his rents, *Macsweyn* was, like other tenants, discontented, and, resigning his farm, removed from *Sky* to *Col*, and was established at *Grissipol*.

These observations we made by favour of the contrary wind that drove us to *Col*, an Island not often visited; for there is not much to amuse curiosity, or to attract avarice.

The ground has been hitherto, I believe, used chiefly for pasturage. In a district, such as the eye can command, there is a general herdsman, who knows all the cattle of the neighbourhood, and whose station is upon a hill, from which he surveys the lower grounds; and if one man's cattle invade another's grass, drives them back to their own borders. But other means of profit begin to be found; kelp is gathered and burnt, and sloops are loaded with the concreted ashes. Cultivation is likely to be improved by the skill and encouragement of the present heir, and the inhabitants of those obscure vallies will partake of the general progress of life.

The rents of the parts which belong to the Duke of Argyle, have been raised from fifty-five to one hundred and five pounds, whether from the land or the sea I cannot tell. The bounties of the sea have lately been so great, that a farm in Southuist has risen in ten years from a rent of thirty pounds to one hundred and eighty.

He who lives in *Col*, and finds himself condemned to solitary

meals, and incommunicable reflection, will find the usefulness of
that middle order of Tacksmen, which some who applaud their own
wisdom are wishing to destroy. Without intelligence man is no
social, he is only gregarious; and little intelligence will there be,
where all are constrained to daily labour, and every mind must wait
upon the hand.

After having listened for some days to the tempest, and wandered
about the Island till our curiosity was satisfied, we began to think
about our departure. To leave *Col* in October is not very easy. We
however found a sloop which lay on the coast to carry kelp; and for
a price which we thought levied upon our necessities, the master
agreed to carry us to *Mull*, whence we might readily pass back to
Scotland.

MULL

As we were to catch the first favourable breath, we spent the night
not very elegantly nor pleasantly in the vessel, and were landed next
day at Tobor Morar, a port in *Mull*, which appears to an unexperi-
enced eye formed for the security of ships; for its mouth is closed by
a small island, which admits them through narrow channels into a
bason sufficiently capacious. They are indeed safe from the sea, but
there is a hollow between the mountains, through which the wind
issues from the land with very mischievous violence.

There was no danger while we were there, and we found several
other vessels at anchor; so that the port had a very commercial
appearance.

The young laird of *Col*, who had determined not to let us lose his
company, while there was any difficulty remaining, came over with
us. His influence soon appeared; for he procured us horses and
conducted us to the house of Doctor *Maclean*, where we found very
kind entertainment, and very pleasing conversation. Miss *Maclean*,
who was born and had been bred at *Glasgow*, having removed with
her father to *Mull*, added to other qualifications, a great knowledge
of the *Earse* language, which she had not learned in her childhood,
but gained by study, and was the only interpreter of *Earse* poetry
that I could ever find.

The Isle of *Mull* is perhaps in extent the third of the Hebrides.
It is not broken by waters, nor shot into promontories, but is a solid
and compact mass, of breadth nearly equal to its length. Of the
dimensions of the larger Islands, there is no knowledge approaching
to exactness. I am willing to estimate it as containing about three
hundred square miles.

Mull has suffered like *Sky* by the black winter of seventy-one, in
which, contrary to all experience, a continued frost detained the
snow eight weeks upon the ground. Against a calamity never known,
no provision had been made, and the people could only pine in

Tobermory from the Daniell print, much as Johnson saw it.

helpless misery. One tenant was mentioned, whose cattle perished to the value of three hundred pounds; a loss which probably more than the life of man is necessary to repair. In countries like these, the descriptions of famine become intelligible. Where by vigorous and artful cultivation of a soil naturally fertile, there is commonly a superfluous growth of both grain and grass; where the fields are crowded with cattle; and where every hand is able to attract wealth from a distance, by making something that promotes ease, or gratifies vanity, a dear year produces only a comparative want, which is rather seen than felt, and which terminates commonly in no worse effect than that of condemning the lower order of the community to sacrifice a little luxury to convenience, or at most a little convenience to necessity.

But where the climate is unkind, and the ground penurious, so that the most fruitful years produce only enough to maintain themselves; where life unimproved, and unadorned, fades into something little more than naked existence, and everyone is busy for himself, without any arts by which the pleasure of others may be increased; if to the daily burden of distress any additional weight be added, nothing remains but to despair and die. In *Mull*, the disappointment of a harvest, or a murrain among the cattle, cuts off the regular provision; and they who have no manufactures can purchase no part of the superfluities of other countries. The consequence of a bad season is here not scarcity, but emptiness; and they whose plenty was barely a supply of natural and present need, when that slender stock fails, must perish with hunger.

All travel has its advantages. If the passenger visits better countries, he may learn to improve his own, and if fortune carries him to worse, he may learn to enjoy it.

Mr. *Boswell's* curiosity strongly impelled him to survey *Iona*, or *Icolmkill*, which was to the early ages the great school of Theology, and is supposed to have been the place of sepulture for the ancient kings. I, though less eager, did not oppose him.

That we might perform this expedition, it was necessary to traverse a great part of *Mull*. We passed a day at Dr. *Maclean's*, and could have been well contented to stay longer. But *Col* provided us horses, and we pursued our journey. This was a day of inconvenience, for the country is very rough, and my horse was but little. We travelled many hours through a tract, black and barren, in which, however, there were the reliques of humanity; for we found a ruined chapel in our way.

It is natural, in traversing this gloom of desolation, to inquire, whether something may not be done to give Nature a more cheerful face, and whether those hills and moors that afford heath cannot with a little care and labour bear something better? The first thought that occurs is to cover them with trees, for that in many of these naked regions trees will grow, is evident, because stumps and roots are yet remaining; and the speculatist hastily proceeds to censure that negligence and laziness that has omitted for so long a time so easy an improvement.

To drop seeds into the ground, and attend their growth, requires little labour and no skill. He who remembers that all the woods by which the wants of man have been supplied from the Deluge till

Despite touches of tar MacAdam the moorland roads of Mull are still pretty awe-inspiring.

Ulva, the traditional home of the
Clan MacQuarrie. Whoever pays
the ferryman, somebody still rings
the bell to summon him.

Inquiring after the reliques of former manners, I found that in
Ulva, and I think no where else, is continued the payment of the
Mercheta Mulierum; a fine in old times due to the Laird at the
marriage of a virgin. The original of this claim, as of our tenure of
Borough English, is variously delivered. It is pleasant to find ancient
customs in old families. This payment, like others, was, for want of
money, made anciently in the produce of the land. *Macquarry* was
used to demand a sheep, for which he now takes a crown, by that
inattention to the uncertain proportion between the value and the
denomination of money, which has brought much disorder into
Europe. A sheep has always the same power of supplying human
wants, but a crown will bring at one time more, at another time
less.

Ulva was not neglected by the piety of ancient times: it has still
to show what was once a church.

INCH KENNETH

In the morning we went again into the boat, and were landed on
Inch Kenneth, an island about a mile long, and perhaps half a mile
broad, remarkable for pleasantness and fertility. It is verdant and
grassy, and fit both for pasture and tillage, but it has no trees. Its
only inhabitants were Sir *Allan Maclean*, and two young ladies, his
daughters, with their servants.

Johnson followed one of the drove roads from Portsonachan to Inveraray. The A819 is less arduous for the modern traveller and traverses beautiful lonely moorland.

Romance does not often exhibit a scene that strikes the imagination more than this little desert in these depths of Western obscurity, occupied not by a gross herdsman, or amphibious fisherman, but by a gentleman and two ladies, of high birth, polished manners, and elegant conversation, who, in a habitation raised not very far above the ground, but furnished with unexpected neatness and convenience, practised all the kindness of hospitality and refinement of courtesy.

Sir *Allan* is the Chieftain of the great Clan of *Maclean*, which is said to claim the second place among the Highland families, yielding only to *Macdonald*. Though by the misconduct of his ancestors, most of the extensive territory, which would have descended to him, has been alienated, he still retains much of the dignity and authority of his birth. When soldiers were lately wanting for the *American* war, application was made to Sir *Allan*, and he nominated a hundred men for the service, who obeyed the summons, and bore arms under his command.

He had then, for some time, resided with the young ladies in *Inch Kenneth*, where he lives not only with plenty, but with elegance, having conveyed to his cottage a collection of books, and what else is necessary to make his hours pleasant.

When we landed, we were met by Sir *Allan* and the ladies, accompanied by Miss *Macquarry*, who had passed some time with them, and now returned to *Ulva* with her father.

We all walked together to the mansion, where we found one cottage for Sir *Allan*, and, I think, two more for the domesticks and the offices. We entered, and wanted little that palaces afford. Our room was neatly floored and well lighted; and our dinner, which was dressed in one of the other huts, was plentiful and delicate.

In the afternoon, Sir *Allan* reminded us that the day was Sunday, which he never suffered to pass without some religious distinction, and invited us to partake in his acts of domestick worship; which I hope neither Mr. *Boswell* nor myself will be suspected of a disposition to refuse. The elder of the ladies read the *English* service.

Inch Kenneth was once a seminary of ecclesiasticks, subordinate, I suppose, to *Icolmkill*. Sir *Allan* had a mind to trace the foundation of the college, but neither I nor Mr. Boswell, who *bends* a keener *eye on vacancy*, were able to perceive them.

Our attention, however, was sufficiently engaged by a venerable chapel, which stands yet entire, except that the roof is gone. It is about sixty feet in length, and thirty in breadth. On one side of the altar is a bas relief of the blessed Virgin, and by it lies a little bell; which, though cracked, and without a clapper, has remained there for ages, guarded only by the venerableness of the place. The ground round the chapel is covered with gravestones of Chiefs and ladies; and still continues to be a place of sepulture.

Inch Kenneth is a proper prelude to *Icolmkill*. It was not without

The ruined chapel on Inchkenneth (aquatint by William Daniell) which moved Boswell to tears.

some mournful emotion that we contemplated the ruins of religious structures, and the monuments of the dead.

On the next day we took a more distinct view of the place, and went with the boat to see oysters in the bed, out of which the boatmen forced up as many as were wanted. Even *Inch Kenneth* has a subordinate Island, named *Sandiland*, I suppose in contempt, where we landed, and found a rock, with a surface of perhaps four acres, of which one is naked stone, another spread with sand and shells, some of which I picked up for their glossy beauty, and two covered with a little earth and grass, on which Sir *Allan* had a few sheep. I doubt not but when there was a college at *Inch Kenneth*, there was a hermitage upon *Sandiland*.

Having wandered over those extensive plains, we committed ourselves again to the winds and waters; and after a voyage of about ten minutes, in which we met with nothing very observable, were again safe upon dry ground.

We told Sir *Allan* our desire of visiting *Icolmkill*, and entreated him to give us his protection, and his company. He thought proper to hesitate a little; but the Ladies hinted, that as they knew he would not finally refuse, he would do better if he preserved the grace of ready compliance. He took their advice, and promised to carry us on the morrow in his boat.

We passed the remaining part of the day in such amusements as were in our power. Sir *Allan* related the *American* campaign, and at evening one of the Ladies played on her harpsichord, while *Col* and Mr. *Boswell* danced a *Scottish* reel with the other.

We could have been easily persuaded to a longer stay upon *Inch Kenneth*, but life will not be all passed in delight. The session at *Edinburgh* was approaching, from which Mr. *Boswell* could not be absent.

In the morning our boat was ready: it was high and strong. Sir

This black house is the kind of 'hut' that Dr Johnson describes. In Auchendrain Museum visitors can see life as it was lived in a West Highland community over the past two hundred years. This is a 'living' museum conducted with immaculate care by curator Bob Smith. Auchendrain escaped the devastation of eviction.

ABOVE

Inveraray Castle is one of the showpiece castles of Scotland. It is the home of the Duke and Duchess of Argyll and it is open to visitors during the summer.

LEFT

The splendid dining room of Inveraray Castle has been beautifully restored (by means of contributions from Campbells from all over the world) after the fire in 1975. The golden galleons transport wine to the guests at the dinner table!

Allan *victualled* it for the day, and provided able rowers. We now parted from the young laird of *Col*, who had treated us with so much kindness, and concluded his favours by consigning us to Sir *Allan*. Here we had the last embrace of this amiable man, who, while these pages were preparing to attest his virtues, perished in the passage between *Ulva* and *Inch Kenneth*.

Sir *Allan*, to whom the whole region was well known, told us of a very remarkable cave, to which he would show us the way. We had been disappointed already by one cave, and were not much elevated by the expectation of another.

It was yet better to see it, and we stopped at some rocks on the coast of *Mull*. The mouth is fortified by vast fragments of stone, over which we made our way, neither very nimbly, nor very securely. The place, however, well repaid our trouble. The bottom, as far as the flood rushes in, was encumbered with large pebbles, but as we advanced was spread over with smooth sand. The breadth is about forty-five feet; the roof rises in an arch, almost regular, to a height which we could not measure; but I think it about thirty feet.

This part of our curiosity was nearly frustrated; for though we went to see a cave, and knew that caves are dark, we forgot to carry tapers, and did not discover our omission till we were wakened by our wants. Sir *Allan* then sent one of the boatmen into the country, who soon returned with one little candle. We were thus enabled to go forward, but could not venture far. Having passed inward from the sea to a great depth, we found on the right hand a narrow passage, perhaps not more than six feet wide, obstructed by great stones, over which we climbed, and came into a second cave, in breadth twenty-five feet. The air in this apartment was very warm, but not oppressive, nor loaded with vapours. Our light showed no tokens of a feculent or corrupted atmosphere. Here was a square stone, called, as we are told, *Fingal's Table*.

If we have been provided with torches, we should have proceeded in our search, though we had already gone as far as any former adventurer, except some who are reported never to have returned; and, measuring our way back, we found it more than a hundred and sixty yards, the eleventh part of a mile.

Our measures were not critically exact, having been made with a walking pole, such as it is convenient to carry in these rocky countries, of which I guessed the length by standing against it. In this there could be no great errour, nor do I much doubt but the Highlander, whom we employed, reported the number right. More nicety however is better, and no man should travel unprovided with instruments for taking heights and distances.

There is yet another cause of errour not always easily surmounted, though more dangerous to the veracity of itinerary narratives, than imperfect mensuration. An observer deeply impressed by any remarkable spectacle, does not suppose, that the traces will soon vanish from his mind, and having commonly no great convenience for writing, defers the description to a time of more leisure, and better accommodation.

He who has not made the experiment, or who is not accustomed to require rigorous accuracy from himself, will scarcely believe how much a few hours take from certainty of knowledge, and distinctness of imagery; how the succession of objects will be broken, how separate parts will be confused, and how many particular features and discriminations will be compressed and conglobated into one gross and general idea.

To this dilatory notation must be imputed the false relations of travellers, where there is no imaginable motive to deceive. They trusted to memory what cannot be trusted safely but to the eye, and told by guess what a few hours before they had known with certainty. Thus it was that *Wheeler* and *Spen* described with irreconcilable contrariety things which they surveyed together, and which both undoubtedly designed to show as they saw them.

When we have satisfied our curiosity in the cave, so far as our penury of light permitted us, we clambered again to our boats, and proceeded along the coast of *Mull* to a headland, called *Atun*, remarkable for the columnar form of the rocks, which rise in a series of pilasters, with a degree of regularity, which Sir *Allan* thinks not less worthy of curiosity than the shore of *Staffa*.

Not long after we came to another range of black rocks, which had the appearance of broken pilasters, set one behind another to a great depth. The place was chosen by Sir *Allan* for our dinner. We were easily accommodated with seats, for the stones were of all heights, and refreshed ourselves and our boatmen, who could have no other rest till we reached *Icolmkill*.

The evening was now approaching, and we were yet a considerable distance from the end of our expedition. We could therefore stop no more to make remarks in the way, but set forward with some degree of eagerness. The day soon failed us, and the moon presented a very solemn and pleasing scene. The sky was clear, so that the eye commanded a wide circle: the sea was neither still nor turbulent: the wind neither silent nor loud. We were never far from one coast or another, on which, if the weather had become violent, we could have found shelter, and therefore contemplated at ease the region through which we glided in the tranquillity of the night, and saw now a rock and now an island grow gradually conspicuous and gradually obscure. I committed the fault which I have just been censuring, in neglecting, as we passed, to note the series of this placid navigation.

We were very near an Island called the *Nun's Island*, perhaps from an ancient convent. Here is said to have been dug the stone which was used in the buildings of *Icolmkill*. Whether it is now inhabited, we could not stay to inquire.

Mackinnon's Cave drawn by Lancelot Speed for George Birbeck Hill. With only one candle Johnson and Boswell were reluctant to venture far into it; photographer Jon Wyand having heard the story of the cave was equally reluctant. Tradition has it that nobody has ever reached its far end and come out again. A piper who went into it in the days when people could interpret the music of the pipes was heard to play 'Woe is me without three hands — two hands for the pipe and one for the sword.' Nobody knows what he needed the sword for because nobody ever saw him again; when his dog reappeared it had lost all its hair.

Loch Fyne, once the great 'herring' loch of Scotland.

The famous old road through Glencroe was ideal for strenuous car rallying, but by the time the pedestrian had negotiated it (since long before cars) he was glad to 'rest and be thankful'.

An efficient motor ferry carries thousands of visitors from Bunessan to Iona nowadays. There is no need to be piggy-backed ashore unless one has kinky ideas of one's own, and such ideas don't flourish on Iona.

At last we came to *Icolmkill*, but found no convenience for landing. Our boat could not be forced very near the dry ground, and our Highlanders carried us over the water.

We were now treading that illustrious Island, which was once the luminary of the *Caledonian* regions, whence savage Clans and roving barbarians derived the benefits of knowledge and the blessings of religion. To abstract the mind from all local emotion would be impossible, if it were endeavoured, and would be foolish if it were possible. Whatever withdraws us from the power of our senses; whatever makes the past, the distant, or the future predominate over the present, advances us in the dignity of thinking beings. Far from me and from my friends, be such frigid philosophy as may conduct us indifferent and unmoved over any ground which has been dignified by wisdom, bravery, or virtue. That man is little to be envied, whose patriotism would not gain force upon the plain of *Marathon*, or whose piety would not grow warmer among the ruins of *Iona*.

We came too late to visit monuments: some care was necessary for ourselves. Whatever was in the Island Sir *Allan* could demand, for the inhabitants were *Macleans*; but having little they could not give us much. He went to the head man of the Island, whom Fame, but Fame delights in amplifying, represents as worth no less than fifty pounds. He was perhaps proud enough of his guests, but ill prepared

Iona Abbey before its restoration, from the print by William Daniell. Johnson himself wrote the most famous appreciation of Iona, and there is no doubt that the island has an atmosphere unequalled even in the Minoan ruins of Crete. Here, in 563, Columba arrived from Ireland with twelve companions seeking a sanctuary from which he could no longer see his beloved Ireland lest he be tempted back to it. And here he built his monastery from which he spread the gospel out to the people of the far north of Scotland and, according to some, as far afield as Iceland. Through the years it became a centre of light and religion and education, and, in time, a hallowed shrine. Over the centuries the Scottish kings, including MacBeth, were buried here.

Many centres of worship were built here, but the ruins shown by Daniell (and seen by Johnson) were the remains of the Benedictine Church which was the cathedral for the See of Argyll till the end of the sixteenth century. The church was gifted to the Church of Scotland by the 8th Duke of Argyll in 1899, and in 1938 the Revd Dr George F. MacLeod (now Lord MacLeod of Fiunary) established the Iona Community which set about the sacred task of restoring the ancient buildings to their present state. It was a labour of piety which breathes of love. In 1979 the present Duke of Argyll sold Iona to the National Trust for 1½ million pounds.

Although thousands of pilgrims visit Iona every summer it has managed to retain its simple unspoilt quality of life. It has a population of under 200 very ordinary people who do everyday work on their crofts and in their fishing boats and enjoy a pint of beer like anybody else!

Lonely Glencroe links Loch Fyne to Loch Long.

Loch Lomond. Its moods change with every twist of the road, and there are many.

for our entertainment; however, he soon produced more provision than men not luxurious require. Our lodging was next to be provided. We found a barn well stocked with hay, and made our beds as soft as we could.

In the morning we rose and surveyed the place. The churches of the two convents are both standing, though unroofed. They were built of unhewn stone, but solid, and not inelegant. I brought away rude measures of the buildings, such as I cannot much trust myself, inaccurately taken, and obscurely noted. Mr. *Pennant's* delineations, which are doubtless exact, have made my unskilful description less necessary.

The episcopal church consists of two parts, separated by the belfry, and built at different times. The original church had, like others, the altar at one end, and tower at the other; but as it grew too small, another building of equal dimension was added, and the tower then was necessarily in the middle.

That these edifices are of different ages seems evident. The arch of the first church is *Roman*, being part of a circle; that of the additional building is pointed, and therefore Gothick, or Saracenical; the tower is firm, and wants only to be floored and covered.

Of the chambers or cells belonging to the monks, there are some walls remaining, but nothing approaching to a complete apartment.

The bottom of the church is so encumbered with mud and rubbish, that we could make no discoveries of curious inscriptions, and what there are have been already published. The place is said to be known where the black stones lie concealed, on which the old Highland Chiefs, when they made contracts and alliances, used to take the oath which was considered as more sacred than any other obligation, and which could not be violated without the blackest infamy. In those days of violence and rapine, it was of great importance to impress upon savage minds the sanctity of an oath, by some particular and extraordinary circumstances. They would not have recourse to the black stones upon small or common occasions, and when they had established their faith by this tremendous sanction, inconstancy and treachery were no longer feared.

The chapel of the nunnery is now used by the inhabitants as a kind of general cow-house, and the bottom is consequently too miry for examination. Some of the stones which covered the later abbesses have inscriptions, which might yet be read if the chapel were cleaned. The roof of this, as of all the other buildings, is totally destroyed, not only because timber quickly decays when it is neglected, but because in an island utterly destitute of wood, it was wanted for use, and was consequently the first plunder of needy rapacity.

The chancel of the nuns' chapel is covered with an arch of stone, to which time has done no injury; and a small apartment communicating with the choir on the north side, like the chapter-house in cathedrals, roofed with stone in the same manner, is likewise entire.

In one of the churches was a marble altar, which the superstition of the inhabitants has destroyed. Their opinion was, that a fragment of this stone was a defence against shipwrecks, fire, and miscarriages. In one corner of the church the bason for holy water is yet unbroken.

The cemetery of the nunnery was, till very lately, regarded with such reverence that only women were buried in it. These reliques of veneration always produce some mournful pleasure. I could have forgiven a great injury more easily than the violation of this imaginary sanctity.

South of the chapel stand the walls of a large room, which was probably the hall or refectory of the nunnery. This apartment is capable of repair. Of the rest of the convent there are only fragments.

Besides the two principal churches, there are, I think, five chapels yet standing, and three more remembered. There are also crosses, of which two bear the names of St. *John* and St. *Matthew*.

A large space of ground about these consecrated edifices is covered with gravestones, few of which have any inscription. He that surveys it, attended by an insular antiquary, may be told where the Kings of many nations are buried, and if he loves to sooth his imagination with the thoughts that naturally rise in places where the great and the powerful lie mingled with the dust, let him listen in submissive silence; for if he asks any questions his delight is at an end.

Iona has long enjoyed, without any very credible attestation, the honour of being reputed the cemetery of the *Scottish* Kings. It is not unlikely, that, when the opinion of local sanctity was prevalent, the Chieftains of the Isles, and perhaps some of the *Norwegian* or *Irish* princes, were reposited in this venerable enclosure. But by whom the subterraneous vaults are peopled is now utterly unknown. The graves are very numerous, and some of them undoubtedly contain the remains of men, who did not expect to be so soon forgotten.

Not far from this awful ground, may be traced the garden of the monastery: the fish-ponds are yet discernible, and the aqueduct, which supplied them, is still in use.

There remains a broken building, which is called the Bishop's house, I know not by what authority. It was once the residence of some man above the common rank, for it has two stories and a chimney. We were shewn a chimney at the other end, which was only a nich, without perforation, but so much does antiquarian credulity or patriotic, vanity prevail, that it is not much more safe to trust the eye of our instructor than the memory.

There is in the Island one house more, and only one, that has a chimney; we entered it, and found it neither wanting repair nor inhabitants; but to the farmers who now possess it, the chimney is of no great value; for their fire was made on the floor, in the middle

Glasgow Cathedral. It escaped the destruction of the Reformation and all denominations can worship in it now. Its foundations go back to the sixth century; its present style to the thirteenth.

The interior of Burns's Cottage in Alloway; more hallowed in the Scottish tradition than 17 Gough Square in that of England!

of the room, and notwithstanding the dignity of their mansion, they rejoiced, like their neighbours, in the comforts of smoke.

It is observed, that ecclesiastical colleges are always in the most pleasant and fruitful places. While the world allowed the monks their choice, it is surely no dishonour that they chose well. The Island is remarkably fruitful. The village near the churches is said to contain seventy families, which, at five in a family, is more than a hundred inhabitants to a mile. There are perhaps other villages; yet both corn and cattle are annually exported.

But the fruitfulness of *Iona* is now its whole prosperity. The inhabitants are remarkably gross, and remarkably neglected: I know not if they are visited by any Minister. The Island, which was once the metropolis of learning and piety, has now no school for education, nor temple for worship, only two inhabitants that can speak *English*, and not one that can write or read.

The people are of the Clan of *Maclean*; and though Sir *Allan* had not been in the place for many years, he was received with all the reverence due their Chieftain. One of them being sharply reprehended by him, for not sending him some rum, declared after his departure, in Mr. *Boswell's* presence, that he had no design of disappointing him, *for,' said he, I would cut my bones for him; and if he had sent his dog for it, he should have had it.*

When we were to depart, our boat was left by the ebb at a great distance from the water, but no sooner did we wish it afloat, than the islanders gathered round it, and, by the union of many hands, pushed it down the beach; every man who could contribute his help seemed to think himself happy in the opportunity of being, for a moment, useful to his Chief.

We now left these illustrious ruins, by which Mr. *Boswell* was much affected, nor would I willingly be thought to have looked upon them without some emotion. Perhaps, in the revolutions of the world, *Iona* may be some time again the instructress of the Western regions.

It was no voyage to *Mull*, where, under Sir *Allan's* protection, we landed in the evening, and were entertained for the night by Mr. *Maclean*, a Minister that lives upon the coast, whose elegance of conversation, and strength of judgment, would make him conspicuous in places of greater celebrity. Next day we dined with Dr. *Maclean*, another physician, and then travelled on to the house of a very powerful Laird, *Maclean* of *Lochbuy*; for in this country every man's name is *Maclean*.

Where races are thus numerous, and thus combined, none but the Chief of a clan is addressed by his name. The Laird of *Dunvegan* is called *Macleod*, but other gentlemen of the same family are denominated by the places where they reside, as *Raasay*, or *Talisker*. The distinction of the meaner people is made by their Christian names. In consequence of this practice, the late Laird of *Macfarlane*, an eminent genealogist, considered himself as disrespectfully treated, if the common addition was applied to him. Mr. *Macfarlane*, said he, "may with equal propriety be said to many; but I, and I only, am Macfarlane."

Our afternoon journey was through a country of such gloomy desolation, that Mr. *Boswell* thought no part of the Highlands equally terrific, yet we came without any difficulty, at evening, to *Lochbuy*, where we found a true Highland Laird, rough and haughty, and tenacious of his dignity; who, hearing my name, inquired whether I was of the *Johnstons of Glencoe*, or of *Ardnamurchan*.

Lochbuy has, like the other insular Chieftains, quitted the castle that sheltered his ancestors, and lives near it, in a mansion not very spacious or splendid. I have seen no houses in the Islands much to be envied for convenience or magnificence, yet they bear testimony to the progress of arts and civility, as they shew that rapine and surprise are no longer dreaded, and are much more commodious than the ancient fortresses.

The castles of the *Hebrides*, many of which are standing and many ruined, were always built upon points of land, on the margin of the sea. For the choice of this situation there must have been some general reason, which the change of manners has left in obscurity. They were of no use in the days of piracy, as defences of the coast; for it was equally accessible in other places. Had they been sea-marks or light-houses, they would have been of more use to the invader than the natives, who could want no such directions on their own waters; for a watch-tower, a cottage on a hill would have been better, as it would have commanded a wider view.

If they be considered merely as places of retreat, the situation seems not well chosen; for the Laird of an Island is safest from foreign enemies in the centre: on the coast he might be more suddenly surprised than in the inland parts; and the invaders, if their enterprise miscarried, might more easily retreat. Some convenience, however, whatever it was, their position on the shore afforded; for uniformity of practice seldom continues long without good reason.

A castle in the Islands is only a single tower of three or four stories, of which the walls are sometimes eight or nine feet thick, with narrow windows, and close winding stairs of stone. The top rises in a cone, or pyramid of stone, encompassed by battlements. The intermediate floors are sometimes frames of timber, as in common houses, and sometimes arches of stone, or alternatively stone and timber; so that there was very little danger from fire. In the center of every floor, from top to bottom, is the chief room, of no great extent, round which there are narrow cavities, or recesses, formed by small vacuities, or by a double wall. I know not whether there be ever more than one fireplace. They had no capacity to contain many people, or much provision; but their enemies could seldom stay to blockade them; for if they failed in the first attack, their next care was to escape.

The walls were always too strong to be shaken by such desultory hostilities; the windows were too narrow to be entered, and the battlements too high to be scaled. The only danger was at the gates, over which the wall was built with a square cavity, not unlike a chimney, continued to the top. Through this hollow the defendants let fall stones upon those who attempted to break the gate, and poured down water, perhaps scalding water, if the attack was made with fire. The castle of *Lochbuy* was secured by double doors, of which the outer was an iron gate.

In every castle is a well and a dungeon. The use of the well is evident. The dungeon is a deep subterraneous cavity, walled on the sides, and arched on the top, into which the descent is through a narrow door, by a ladder or rope, so that it seems impossible to escape, when the rope or ladder is drawn up. The dungeon was, I suppose, in war, a prison for such captives as were treated with severity, and, in peace for such delinquents as had committed crimes within the Laird's jurisdiction; for the mansion of many Lairds were, till the late privation of their privileges, the halls of justice to their own tenants.

As these fortifications were the productions of mere necessity, they are built only for safety, with little regard to convenience, and with none to elegance or pleasure. It was sufficient for a laird of the *Hebrides*, if he had a strong house, in which he could hide his wife

The original Castle of Moy was abandoned by the Maclaine Chiefs in 1752. Johnson's flamboyant host, John, the 17th Chief, refused to accept that the Highland Chiefs had lost 'the power of pit and gallows' in 1747 and he had been heavily fined in the Court of Session for imprisoning two of his tenants in the dungeons. Boswell's father had been one of the presiding judges — a fact which their host kept bringing up, to Boswell's embarrassment. The Maclaines were great monument-builders, and tourists find plenty to interest them in the Lochbuie area.

Duart Castle in Mull – dark sentinel of the Sound of Mull; the traditional home of the Chiefs of Clan Maclean. Johnson and Boswell didn't call at Duart; it was in ruins at the time, having been burnt by the Duke of Argyll in 1691. The Macleans fought with Prince Charlie in 1745 and, as a result, their property including the castle was confiscated. It was repossessed and restored to an elegant family home by Sir Fitzroy Maclean, the Chief of the time, in 1912, and it has been a family home ever since.

and children from the next Clan. That they are not large nor splendid is no wonder. It is not easy to find how they are raised, such as they are, by men who had no money, in countries where the labourers and artificers could scarcely be fed. The buildings in different parts of the Islands show their degrees of wealth and power. I believe that for all the castle which I have seen beyond the Tweed, the ruins yet remaining of some one of these which the English built in Wales, would supply materials.

These castles afford another evidence that the fictions of romantick chivalry had for their basis the real manners of the feudal times, when every Lord of a seignory lived in his hold lawless and unaccountable, with all the licentiousness and insolence of uncontested superiority and unprincipled power. The traveller, whoever he might be, coming to the fortified habitation of a Chieftain, would probably have been interrogated from the battlements, admitted with caution at the gate, introduced to a petty Monarch, fierce with habitual hostility, and vigilant with ignorant suspicion; who, according to his general temper or accidental humour, would have seated a stranger as his guest at the table, or as a spy confined him in the dungeon.

Lochbuy means the *Yellow Lake*, which is the name given to an inlet of the sea upon which the castle of Mr. *Maclean* stands. The reason of the appellation we did not learn.

We were now to leave the *Hebrides*, where we had spent some weeks with sufficient amusement, and where we had amplified our thoughts with new scenes of nature, and new modes of life. More

Oban in 1791 as seen by Thomas Newte. Then, as during Johnson's brief visit, the town was a tiny village of fishermen's houses and a tolerable inn. If Johnson were visiting the Inner Hebrides today he would probably make Oban his base; at least thousands of others do every summer. It is a beautiful town, with a harbour landlocked by the island of Kerrera. Its crowning glory is MacCaig's Folly built by a wealthy businessman in 1890 to provide work for the unemployed people of the town.

Oban has a population of 6, 500 in winter; it multiplies hugely in summer but one is happily not too much aware of it because tourists tend to take themselves elsewhere if the weather is reasonable. The town was the capital of the Clan MacDougall from the seventh century onwards till they were taken over by the Campbells. The MacDougall castle, Dunollie, is now a ruin, but the most charming of Clan Chiefs, Madame Coline MacDougall of MacDougall, still lives in the town; she is the proud possessor of the priceless Brooch of Lorne which some of her clansfolk obtained when they nearly captured Robert Bruce in the early fourteenth century and, thereby, almost altered the entire course of Scottish history.

Boswell House in Oban now stands on the site of the tolerable inn *where Johnson stayed when he got ashore.*

time would have given us a more distinct view, but it was necessary that Mr. *Boswell* should return before the courts of justice were opened; and it was not proper to live too long upon hospitality, however liberally imparted.

Of these islands it must be confessed that they have not many allurements, but to the mere lover of naked nature. The inhabitants are thin, provisions are scarce, and desolation and penury give little pleasure.

The people, collectively considered, are not few, though their numbers are small in proportion to the space which they occupy. *Mull* is said to contain six thousand, and *Sky* fifteen thousand. Of the computation respecting *Mull* I can give no account; but when I doubted the truth of the numbers attributed to *Sky*, one of the ministers exhibited such facts as conquered my incredulity.

Of the proportion, which the product of any region bears to the people, an estimate is commonly made according to the pecuniary price of the necessaries of life; a principle of judgment which is never certain, because it supposes what is far from truth, that the value of money is always the same, and so measures an unknown quantity by an uncertain standard. It is competent enough when the markets of the same country, at different times, and those times not too distant, are to be compared; but of very little use for the purpose of making one nation acquainted with the state of another. Provisions, though plentiful, are sold in places of great pecuniary opulence for nominal prices, to which, however scarce, where gold and silver are yet scarcer, they can never be raised.

In the *Western Islands* there is so little internal commerce, that hardly any thing has a known or settled rate. The price of things brought in, or carried out, is to be considered as that of a foreign market; and even this there is some difficulty in discovering, because their denominations of quantity are different from ours; and when there is ignorance on both sides, no appeal can be made to a common measure.

This, however, is not the only impediment. The *Scots*, with a vigilance of jealousy which never goes to sleep, always suspect that an *Englishman* despises them for their poverty, and to convince him that they are not less rich than their neighbours, are sure to tell him a price higher than the true. When *Lesley*, two hundred years ago, related so punctiliously that a hundred hen-eggs, new-laid, were sold in the Islands for a penny, he supposed that no inference could possibly follow, but that the eggs were in great abundance. Posterity has since grown wiser; and having learned, that nominal and real value may differ, they now tell no such stories, lest the foreigner should happen to collect, not that eggs are many, but that pence are few.

Money and wealth have, by the use of commercial language been so long confounded, that they are commonly supposed to be the

Inveraray in 1820. The dazzling white frontage of Inveraray on Loch Fyne makes it an unforgettably attractive town on first viewing, and although it retains very little of its ancient past it still has an atmosphere that is almost tangible.

The town is the oldest in Argyll and there is no trace of its earliest records beyond that it was built round an old Clan Campbell castle. As it stands today Inveraray is a good example of an early 'planned' town, finally built around 1750. The 3rd Duke of Argyll had originally planned to move the whole of old Inveraray village to surround the new castle which he built a mile to the north of the old one (1746–82), but, thankfully for the sake of the town and the new castle, artistic sense prevailed. Inveraray has a population of only 500 or so and it hasn't developed as a major tourist centre because the overwhelming attraction of the area is the great castle itself which is a mecca for the day-tripper, to whom it is open for the summer months.

Inveraray has been the capital of Clan Campbell since they embarked on their great expansionsist policies and left Inchchonail on Lochawe at the end of the fifteenth century. Since then the Campbells of Argyll have been the wealthiest and the most successful of all the Highland clans by dint of being, for most of the

time, on the right side of the Government in power and by the art of their Chiefs marrying women who were beautiful and rich and well connected.

The present castle of Inveraray (which was in process of being completed when it was visited by Johnson) is not necessarily the most architecturally tasteful in Scotland; it tends to look faintly like a fairy castle moulded out of grey blancmange. But, inside, it is breathtaking. Its rooms (now restored after a disastrous fire in 1975) are magnificently decorated and lit by hundredweights of crystal chandeliers. Its treasures include one of the best libraries in Britain, eighteenth century Beauvais tapestry, Japanese Imari ware, magnificent period furniture immaculately matched, and paintings which include works by Gainsborough, Batoni, Raeburn and the rest. The present Duke (the 12th) is an electronics engineer by profession and a brilliant businessman; he claims to have no money, by which he probably means that he has no change in his pocket at that precise moment!

Boswell was ill at ease during their visit to Inverary; he had just been involved in his professional capacity, in a suit against the Duke of Argyll, and the Duchess (the beautiful Elizabeth Gunning) made him squirm more by what she did not say than by anything she said.

Johnson crossed Loch Awe to
Portsonochan on his way from
Oban to Inveraray. It is now
impossible to decide which drove
track he followed even if one
wanted to retrace it. Jon Wyand's
route is near enough for the
average traveller, and saves him
having to ford the innumerable
burns of which Johnson lost count.

same; and this prejudice has spread so widely in *Scotland*, that I
know not whether I found man or woman, whom I interrogated
concerning payments of money, that could surmount the illiberal
desire of deceiving me, by representing everything as dearer than it
is.

From *Lochbuy* we rode a very few miles to the side of *Mull* which
faces *Scotland*, where, having taken leave of our kind protector, Sir
Allan, we embarked in a boat, in which the seat provided for our
accommodation was a heap of rough brushwood; and on the twenty-
second of *October* reposed at a tolerable inn on the main land.

On the next day we began our journey southwards. The weather
was tempestuous. For half the day the ground was rough, and our
horses were still small. Had they required much restraint, we might
have been reduced to difficulties; for I think we had amongst us but
one bridle. We fed the poor animals liberally, and they performed
their journey well. In the latter part of the day, we came to a firm
and smooth road, made by the soldiers, on which we travelled with
great security, busied with contemplating the scene about us. The
night came on while we had yet a great part of the way to go, though
not so dark but that we could discern the cataracts which poured
down the hills, on one side, and fell into one general channel that
ran with great violence on the other. The wind was loud, the rain
was heavy, and the whistling of the blast, the fall of the shower, the
rush of the cataracts, and the roar of the torrent, make a nobler
chorus of the rough musick of nature than it had ever been my
chance to hear before. The streams which ran cross the way from the

The Hall of Inveraray Castle with its remarkable 'collage' of armoury.

Glencroe, despite its excellent road now, is one of the eeriest glens in Scotland – almost as much so as Glencoe with which some Johnson writers have confused it. Glencroe lies between Loch Fyne and Loch Lomond, and it was here that Johnson saw the stone carved 'Rest and be thankful'. It is still there, though the detailed inscription was made some time after Johnson's visit.

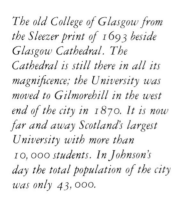

The old College of Glasgow from the Sleezer print of 1693 beside Glasgow Cathedral. The Cathedral is still there in all its magnificence; the University was moved to Gilmorehill in the west end of the city in 1870. It is now far and away Scotland's largest University with more than 10,000 students. In Johnson's day the total population of the city was only 43,000.

hills to the main current, were so frequent that after a while I began to count them; and in ten miles reckoned fifty-five, probably missing some, and having let some pass before they forced themselves upon my notice. At last we came to *Inverary*, where we found an inn, not only commodious, but magnificent.

The difficulties of peregrination were now at an end. Mr. *Boswell* had the honour of being known to the Duke of *Argyle*, by whom we were very kindly entertained at his splendid seat, and supplied with conveniences for surveying his spacious park and rising forests.

After two days' stay at *Inverary* we proceeded southward over *Glencroe*, a black and dreary region, made easily passable by a military road, which rises from either end of the *glen* by an acclivity not dangerously steep, but sufficiently laborious. In the middle, at the top of the hill, is a seat with this inscription, *Rest and be thankful*. Stones were placed to mark the distances, which the inhabitants have taken away, resolved, they said, *to have no new miles*.

In this rainy season the hills streamed with waterfalls, which, crossing the way, formed currents on the other side, that ran in contrary directions as they fell to the north or south of the summit. Being, by favour of the Duke, well mounted, I went up and down the hill with great convenience.

From *Glencroe* we passed through a pleasant country to the banks of *Loch Lomond*, and were received at the house of Sir *James Colquhoun*, who is owner of almost all the thirty islands of the Loch, which we went in a boat to survey. The heaviness of the rain shortened our voyage, but we landed on one island planted with yew, and stocked with deer, and on another containing not more perhaps than half an acre, remarkable for the ruins of an old castle, on which the osprey

builds her annual nest. Had *Loch Lomond* been in a happier climate, it would have been the boast of wealth and vanity to own one of the little spots which it incloses, and to have employed upon it all the arts of embellishment. But as it is, the islets, which court the gazer at a distance, disgust him at his approach, when he finds, instead of soft lawns and shady thickets, nothing more than uncultivated ruggedness.

A view of Glasgow in 1820, forty years before the real population explosion took place.

Where the Loch discharges itself into a river called the *Leven*, we passed a night with Mr. *Smollett*, a relation to Dr. *Smollett*, to whose memory he has raised an obelisk on the bank near the house in which he was born. The civility and respect which we found at every place, it is ungrateful to omit, and tedious to repeat. Here we were met by a post-chaise that conveyed us to *Glasgow*.

To describe a city so much frequented as Glasgow is unnecessary. The prosperity of its commerce appears in the greatness of many private houses, and a general appearance of wealth. It is the only episcopal city whose cathedral was left standing in the rage of the Reformation. It is now divided into many separate places of worship, which, taken all together, compose a great pile, that had been some centuries in building, but was never finished; for the change of religion intercepted its progress before the cross isle was added, which seems essential to a *Gothick* cathedral.

The college has not had a sufficient share of the increasing magnificence of the place. The session was begun for it commences on the tenth of *October* and continues to the tenth of *June*, but the students appeared not numerous, being, I suppose, not yet returned from their several homes. The division of the academical year into one session, and one recess, seems to me better accommodated to

Auchinleck House which Boswell's father had newly built when Johnson spent an uneasy few days there. He described it as magnificent and convenient *but felt it didn't have the character of the castle. The new house itself is now closed down and in disrepair.*

the present state of life than variegation of time by terms and vacations, derived from distant centuries, in which it was probably convenient, and still continued in *English* Universities. So many solid months as the *Scotch* scheme of education joins together, allow and encourage a plan for each part of the year; but with us, he that has settled upon himself to study in the college is soon tempted into the country, and he that has adjusted his life in the country, is summoned back to his college.

Yet when I have allowed to the Universities of *Scotland* a more rational distribution of time, I have given them, so far as my inquiries have informed me, all that they can claim. The students, for the most part, go thither boys, and depart before they are men; they carry with them little fundamental knowledge, and therefore the superstructure cannot be lofty. The grammar schools are not generally well supplied; for the character of a schoolmaster being there less honourable than in *England*, is seldom accepted by men who are capable to adorn it, and where the school has been deficient, the college can effect little.

Men bred in the universities of *Scotland* cannot be expected to be often decorated with the splendours of ornamental erudition, but

they obtain a mediocrity of knowledge, between learning and ignorance, not inadequate to the purposes of common life, which is, I believe, very widely diffused among them, and which, countenanced in general by a national combination so invidious, that their friends cannot defend it, and actuated in particulars by a spirit of enterprise, so vigorous, that their enemies are constrained to praise it, enables them to find, or make their way to employment, riches, and distinction.

From *Glasgow* we directed our course to *Auchinleck*, an estate devolved, through a long series of ancestors, to Mr. *Boswell's* father, the present possessor. In our way we found several places remarkable enough in themselves, but already described by those who viewed them at more leisure, or with much more skill; and stopped two days at Mr. *Campbell's*, a gentleman married to Mr. *Boswell's* sister.

Auchinleck, which signifies a *stony field*, seems not now to have any particular claim to its denomination. It is a district generally level and sufficiently fertile, but, like all the *Western* side of *Scotland*, incommoded by very frequent rain. It was, with the rest of the country, generally naked, till the present possessor finding, by the growth of some stately trees near his old castle, that the ground was favourable enough to timber, adorned it very diligently with annual plantations.

Lord *Auchinleck*, who is one of the judges of *Scotland*, and therefore not wholly at leisure for domestick business or pleasure, has yet found time to make improvements in his patrimony. He has built a house of hewn stone, very stately, and durable, and has advanced the value of his lands with great tenderness to his tenants.

I was, however, less delighted with the elegance of the modern

Although not on the Johnson *trail few visitors to Ayrshire will fail to visit Burns's cottage in Alloway. It is perhaps fanciful to suppose that, even had his sight been better, Johnson would have noticed a 14-year-old ploughboy whose name would one day rival or even eclipse his own, and give a new dimension to vernacular literature.*

mansion, than with the sullen dignity of the old castle. I clambered with Mr. *Boswell* among the ruins, which afford striking images of ancient life. It is, like other castles, built upon a point of rock, and was, I believe, anciently surrounded with a moat. There is another rock near to it, to which the drawbridge, when it was let down, is said to have reached. Here, in the ages of tumult and rapine, the Laird was surprised and killed by the neighbouring Chief, who perhaps might have extinguished the family, had he not in a few days been seized and hanged, together with his sons, by *Douglas*, who came with his forces to the relief of *Auchinleck*.

At no great distance from the house runs a pleasing brook, by a red rock, out of which has been hewn a very agreeable and commodious summerhouse, at less expense, as Lord *Auchinleck* told me, than would have been required to build a room of the same dimensions. The rock seems to have no more dampness than any other wall. Such opportunities of variety it is judicious not to neglect.

We now returned to *Edinburgh*, where I passed some days with men of learning, whose names want no advancement from my commemoration, or with women of elegance, which perhaps disclaims a pedant's praise.

The conversation of the *Scots* grows every day less unpleasing to the *English*; their peculiarities wear fast away; their dialect is likely to become in half a century provincial and rustic, even to themselves. The great, the learned, the ambitious, and the vain, all cultivate the *English* phrase, and the *English* pronunciation, and in splendid companies *Scotch* is not much heard, except now and then from an old Lady.

There is one subject of philosophical curiosity to be found in *Edinburgh*, which no other city has to shew; a college of the deaf and dumb, who are taught to speak, to read, to write, and to practise arithmetick, by a gentleman, whose name is *Braidwood*. The number which attends him is, I think, about twelve, which he brings together into a little school, and instructs according to their several degrees of proficiency.

I do not mean to mention the instruction of the deaf as new. Having been first practised upon the son of a constable of *Spain*, it was afterwards cultivated with much emulation in England, by *Wallis* and *Holder*, and was lately professed by Mr. *Baker*, who once flattered me with hopes of seeing his method published. How far any former teachers have succeeded, it is not easy to know; the improvement of Mr. *Braidwood's* pupils is wonderful. They not only speak, write, and understand what is written, but if he that speaks looks towards them, and modifies his organs by distinct and full utterance, they know so well what is spoken, that it is an expression scarcely figurative to say, they hear with the eye. That any have attained to the power, mentioned by *Burnet*, of feeling sounds, by

Johnson was weary by the time he arrived back in Edinburgh on 10 November and he would willingly have headed back for London. But Boswell would have none of it and the old man had to spend ten more days at Boswell's house in James's Court where, presumably, Mrs Boswell had to surrender her marital bed to her guest once again. By now she was fed up with his idiosyncrasies – his irregular hours and his uncouth habits such as turning the candles upside down when they didn't burn brightly enough and letting the wax drop on to the carpets – and she was scunnered by her husband's fawning. 'I have seen many a bear led by a man; but I never before saw a man led by a bear.'

Johnson himself had to put up with a murderous schedule of visits to the homes of the Edinburgh literati and socialites, than whom there is no more tiring brigade. 'Sir,' he moaned 'we have been harassed by invitations.' And when he had a morning in the house while Boswell was at the law courts he had 'a constant levee of various persons of very different character and descriptions' while Mrs Boswell was left 'to the endless task of pouring out tea'.

The beleaguered visitor was not insensitive to the atmosphere in James's Court; when he wrote to Boswell from London after his return he said rather plaintively 'I know Mrs Boswell wished me well to go; her wishes have not been disappointed.' And James Boswell could not but privately concur.

laying a hand on the speaker's mouth, I know not; but I have seen so much, that I can believe more; a single word, or a short sentence, I think, may possibly be so distinguished.

It will readily be supposed by those that consider this subject, that Mr. *Braidwood's* scholars spell accurately. Orthography is vitiated among such as learn first to speak, and then to write, by imperfect notions of the relation between letters and vocal utterance; but to those students every character is of equal importance; for letters are to them not symbols of names, but of things; when they write they do not represent a sound, but delineate a form.

This school I visited, and found some of the scholars waiting for their master, whom they are said to receive at his entrance with smiling countenances and sparkling eyes, delighted with the hope of new ideas. One of the young Ladies had her slate before her, on which I wrote a question consisting of three figures, to be multiplied by two figures. She looked upon it, and quivering her fingers in a manner which I thought very pretty, but of which I know not whether it was art or play, multiplied the sum regularly in two lines, observing the decimal place; but did not add the two lines together, probably disdaining so easy an operation. I pointed at the place where the sum total should stand, and she noted it with such expedition as seemed to shew that she had it only to write.

It was pleasing to see one of the most desperate of human calamities capable of so much help; whatever enlarges hope, will exalt courage; after having seen the deaf taught arithmetick, who would be afraid to cultivate the *Hebrides*?

Such are the things which this journey has given me an opportunity of seeing, and such are the reflections which that sight has raised. Having passed my time almost wholly in cities, I may have been surprised by modes of life and appearances of nature that are familiar to men of wider survey and more varied conversation. Novelty and ignorance must always be reciprocal, and I cannot but be conscious that my thoughts on national manners, are the thoughts of one who has seen but little.

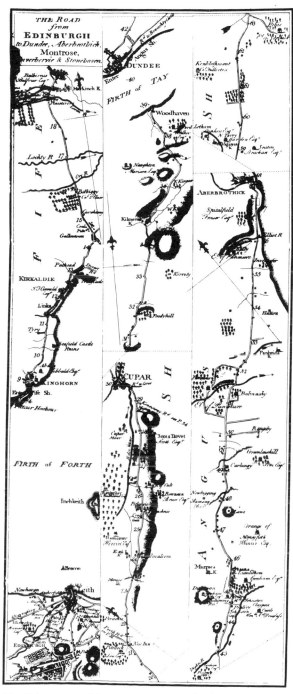

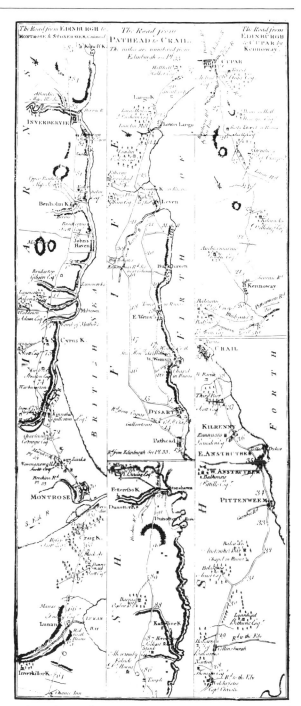

Dr Johnson would not require maps for his journey because he was 'handed on' from one contact of Boswell's or his own to another. For example, William Nairne accompanied them as far as St Andrews.

Where they did not have contacts, guides were readily provided — sometimes unlikely ones. At Laurencekirk Johnson was surprised to find that Lord Monboddo had a black manservant — Gory — who was sent to set them

on the right road to Aberdeen. For some reason Johnson had decided to leave his own black servant — the faithful Francis Barber — behind in London.

(All in all the travellers were probably safer with guides than trusting maps of the complexity of these. Apart altogether from the fact that the two examples shown were not published till 1776!)

Random Clarifications

(With apologies to those who already know)

Dr Johnson himself said 'a man will turn over half a library to make one book' and, in the preparation of this *treatment* (any more precise word would be pretentious), I have had the advantage of access to whole libraries of books about Johnson, each book of which, in turn, had ingested libraries of other people's work and researches. Most frequently my forays into tomes of reference were not for deep or subtle interpretations of philosophical points — which interpretations themselves I would almost certainly find beyond me — but rather for simple explanations of things, places and people which humility made me feel I ought to know or immodesty made me feel I had forgotten. Frequently the answers that I found forced on me the conviction that what I had, and had in plenty, was the failing that Dr Johnson himself was humble enough to confess to when the lady asked him why, in his dictionary, he defined *pastern* as *the knee of a horse* — 'Ignorance, madam, pure ignorance.'

In choosing the following list of items for explanation I am perfectly well aware that I am risking insulting many readers who, every morning, refer to *succedaneous means* when they use saccharine instead of sugar in their coffee, or those who habitually leaf through *Prideaux's Connection* before switching off their bedside lamps. Such people can jump to the final section of this volume or, better still, return to the beginning of the *Journey* itself — an exercise which offers new and greater pleasures the more often it is repeated.

Let nobody be discouraged by the thought that the shortness of this list is in any way inversely commensurate with the present writer's knowledge or even remotely reflective of the number of times that he had to refer to those other authorities for enlightenment. The embarrassment that a full cataloguing of such references would have caused, has been spared by the strict apportioning of space by the publishers.

There may be several reasons why Dr Johnson doesn't dwell on the three full days that he spent in Edinburgh before setting off on his journey apart from his tactful claim that it was 'a city too well known to admit description'. For a start he had, at that time, no intention of writing a book and probably didn't make much mental note of what he heard or saw; Boswell had involved him in a social whirl which would have daunted a young man freshly arrived from London by train let alone a 63-year-old heavyweight who had made the journey by horse and cart; he was staying with a woman (Boswell's wife) who had gone out of her way to make him welcome but had steadily 'gone off him' as the days went by and made no secret of the fact. All that and Boswell's eternal chatter . . . Little wonder that poor Johnson, in the second paragraph, could only recall that he had been accompanied out of Edinburgh by

'another gentleman' (p. 15) whose name, presumably, he couldn't remember even although he liked him very much. He was, in fact, *William* Nairne, an advocate who was in later life to become Lord Dunsinnan, a judge of the Court of Session.

'Inch Keith' (p. 15) is, as Johnson describes it, a small island in the Firth of Forth. Up till the early seventeenth century it was invaluable as a fortress protecting the entrance to the Firth. Its claims to fame include the facts that Johnson had visited it and that the Northern Lighthouse Board had, till recently, a manned lighthouse on it. Johnson's dream of it as an island paradise has been realized by Mr Tom Farmer, who has made a fortune out of motor car exhaust systems and has bought it from the Lighthouse Board presumably as a haven from the car polluted city. It was on Inchkeith that James IV had incarcerated two infants in the sole care of a dumb nurse to find out what languages they would speak. Johnson's comment would have been interesting on the finding that 'they spak guid Hebrew'. So might the comment of Hyam MacCoby.

'St Andrews' (p. 17ff). Scotland's most beautiful city, blending the two great civilizations of University learning and golf. As a high Anglican Johnson couldn't fail to be incensed by the desecration of the cathedral, the churches and the monasteries during the Reformation, and his strictures on John Knox are understandable. St Leonard's College, the passing of which Johnson bemoaned, has now been largely reconstituted as St Leonards Girls' School which took over the site in 1882. Had the old man been alive today he would most certainly be at the very least a patron of the St Andrews Preservation Trust which is making a spectacular success of reconstruction and blending old with new. At St Andrews Dr Johnson noted the office of the University's Lord Rector, and the novelty of it appealed to him. It was (and is) a unique office. The Lord Rector is the lay chairman of the University Court at all Scottish Universities; he is the representative of the students, democratically elected by the students; it used to be one of the greatest honours that the student body could confer on people who had made outstanding contributions to society but there is now an increasing tendency for the incumbents to be comedians in some field or other.

'Aberbrothick' (p. 22ff) – now Arbroath. As a staunch Tory (albeit with Jacobite sympathies) it would be uncharacteristic of Johnson to note that it was in this famous Abbey that Scotland's great Declaration of Independence was signed in 1320.

'Lord Monboddo' **(p. 25).** James Burnett (1714–1799). The meeting with Dr Johnson was more successful than Boswell had dared hope, and, in fact, Monboddo went out of his way to meet Johnson again after the latter had returned from the Western Isles. Monboddo was noted for his eccentric (of its time) theory that men were descended from apes, and was prepared to state that men still lived who had tails. In the ordinary course of events he would have been more at home with David Attenborough than with Samuel Johnson. Thanks to Johnson's unwitting propaganda, Monboddo House was surrounded by an elegance of new trees when it was visited by George Birbeck Hill in 1889, but after the First World War it began to fall into disrepair as the fortunes of the Burnett family declined. However, it was acquired recently by a wealthy oil entrepreneur, Mr Tom Fox, who has restored it and now calls it Monboddo Castle.

'Old Aberdeen and New Aberdeen' **(p. 27ff).** Old Aberdeen was partially destroyed by King Edward III in 1336. The town which was rebuilt was called New Aberdeen, but the two distinct divisions still survive, with King's College (the original University) still in the Old Town, and the glorious Marischal College in the New Town although both are now, of course, joined in the same University. Aberdeen has managed to retain much of its clean air and granite splendour although it is now surpassingly rich as the great North Sea Oil capital. Johnson would now find the inns not only very full but very expensive.

'Arthur Johnston' **(p. 29)** (1587–1641) – born in Aberdeenshire and graduated as a doctor of medicine in Padua. He was appointed Royal Physician to King Charles I but it was his fame as a Latin poet that attracted Johnson to his work; he had, among other things, made a famous translation of the Psalms into Latin. Johnson visited two bookshops in Aberdeen searching for a copy of his works but without success.

'A rock perpendicularly tubulated' **(p. 32)** could only be a Johnsonian description of the Bullers of Buchan; the rest of us would call it a tall rock with a hole down the middle. One forever wonders at the overweight 63-year-old myopic scholar scrambling over places like the Bullers of Buchan and Inchkeith while totally ignoring somewhere like Culloden which was still very fresh indeed in the British (far less Highland) memory, or the Cuillin Hills in Skye!

'Streichton' **(p. 34)** doesn't feature in any of the innumerable guide books and gazetteers which owe their proliferation so much to Johnson's own journey. He is probably referring to Strichen (Boswell's references would support this). In addition to all his other ailments Johnson was beginning to go deaf at this stage, and his reproduction

of place names is not always dependable even although he had the advantage of vetting Boswell's journal from time to time. Of course, at this stage he still had no intention of writing a book.

'*Nairn*' (**p. 39**). It was here that Johnson heard 'Erse' for the first time and saw his first peat fire and, not unreasonably, took that as proof that he was now entering the Highlands proper. The Revd Donald McNicol took grave exception to the fact that Johnson referred to Gaelic as 'Erse' but, in fact, Irish Gaelic and Scottish Gaelic had only begun to divide into separate though closely related languages in the sixteenth century, and in 1773 the two languages were still very similar. In 1773 about 90 per cent of the population of the Highlands were monoglot Gaelic speakers, but a ruthless policy of repression of the language had been in force since 1745; it was a policy that was to persist in one way or another for a century and a half. Today the number of Gaelic speakers is about 80,000.

'*Deliciae Poëtarum Scotorum*' (**p. 46**) sounds slightly like a rhyming haggis but it was, in fact, an anthology of Latin poetry by Scottish writers, collected in 1637 by that same Arthur Johnston mentioned above. Johnson had an astonishing knowledge of Scottish literature and a high regard for most of it; in fact one suspects that much of his avowed anti-Scottishness was more 'tongue in cheek' than is often supposed.

'*Lough Ness*' (**p. 49ff**). By the time Johnson had reached Loch Ness he had run out of roads, and the next many miles of his journey were to be on horseback, on foot or by open boat. No less puzzling than his ignoring of Culloden is the fact that no mention of the Loch Monster can have been made to him. Nobody with his interest in anything savouring of the 'extra-terrestrial' could have failed to comment on a phenomenon which has mysteriously and occasionally advantageously haunted Loch Ness since the days of St Columba. What would his reaction have been? Probably the same as to the suggestion of the existence of a ghost, 'All argument is against it; but all belief is for it.' And so say most of us.

'*Fort Augustus*' (**pp. 54–5**). Johnson was hospitably entertained at both the Forts that he visited (Fort George and Fort Augustus), so it behoved him to brush lightly over the reason for their existence. They were there to subjugate the Highlands and expeditions from them did so frequently with brutal efficiency. (So with many of the roads that Johnson travelled; they had been 'cut by *soldiers*' in order to afford government troops greater mobility.) Fort Augustus itself had been built after the 1715 Rising and strengthened after the

Forty-Five. Today it is a Benedictine Monastery with an excellent boarding school attached to it.

'*Glenmollison*' (p. 55). He means Glenmoriston; his hearing was still troubling him – or else the Highland accent. It would be astonishing to find a copy of *Prideaux's Connection* in Glenmoriston today, although one might be surprised.

'*Prideaux's Connection*' (p. 56) was, in fact, a history of the Jews by one Humphrey Prideaux in which he compared the Old Testament and the New. In Glenmoriston Dr Johnson yet again expresses pleased surprise at the pleasant accents of the English-speaking Highlanders that he met, and he attributes this to the civilizing influence of the military! It doesn't occur to him that these people were learning their English and not just picking it up casually in the dubious environs of Bow Bells or the River Clyde.

'*Glenelg*' (p. 68). Johnson must have remembered Glenelg and its environments with very mixed feelings. There was the hospitality of Murdo Murchison (not Gordon as stated) who was, the traveller might have been interested to know, a descendant of one of the early Reformation ministers in those parts. The inn at Glenelg is now restored as the private house seen on p. 81, but wherever one takes bed and breakfast in that part of the world today it is highly unlikely that he will find 'a dirty fellow jumping out of the bed in which one is expected to lie'! (That is roughly how Johnson described the incident to Mrs Thrale. Rather wisely he elected to sleep in his riding coat on a bundle of hay.)

'*Lord Hardwicke*' (p. 72) – not one of the best loved names in the Scottish Highlands. He was the Lord Chancellor at the time of the Forty-Five and the architect of the Prohibition Act banning Highland dress and the Bagpipe, and discouraging the use of Gaelic. He was also involved in the Disarmament Act about which Dr Johnson had a heated argument with his host, Sir Alexander Macdonald, at Armadale. (The better account of this bitter argument is in Boswell's *Journal of the Tour*.)

'*skalk*' (p. 75) – the Gaelic word *sgailc*. In Old Gaelic it meant a large whisky or a dram; in modern Gaelic it means a sharp blow. In either Gaelic a dram of eighteenth-century raw whisky – 'empyreumatic' or no – first thing in the morning must have been an uppercut to the toughest constitution.

'*Raasay*' (p. 77ff). The island was savaged for its support of Prince Charlie but the houses had been rebuilt by the time Johnson and Boswell visited it. The MacLeods of Raasay (Johnson's hosts) and their heirs were excellent landlords and didn't rack-rent or otherwise oppress their tenants. Probably as a result they themselves fell into financial hardship and were forced to sell Raasay in the 1840s. The subsequent history of Raasay has been a tragic one of absentee landlordism, exploitation and neglect, culminating in the recent ruination of the island by the notorious Dr Green. Most of the island has now been taken over by the Department of Agriculture for Scotland and the Highlands and Islands Development Board. Dr Johnson (so often accused of boorishness and insensitivity to the feelings of others) revelled in the hospitality of the MacLeods of Raasay and he was mortified to discover that he had hurt MacLeod by implying, in the first edition of the *Journey* that the MacLeods of Raasay were subordinate to the Chief of Dunvegan. Dr Johnson would not wait to make a correction in the second edition but insisted on publishing an apology in an Edinburgh newspaper.

'Flora Macdonald' (p. 90). Again it's a puzzlement how little Johnson makes of his meeting with the woman who was one of the celebrities of history, far less of her age. Nothing could be less 'Russell Harty' than the way he dismisses his encounter with her. And yet they got on well. One wonders if he ever heard of her adventures in later life – her emigration to America, the involvement of her husband and five sons in the American Civil War and her lonely return to Kingsburgh when her husband was taken prisoner and two of her sons killed. She died in 1790 and is buried in Kilmuir – a few miles north of Kingsburgh. Legend has it that her shroud was the sheet in which Prince Charlie had slept at Kingsburgh 11 years earlier.

'Ostig' (p. 103) or Ostaig (which is dealt with separately on p. 104) is the nub and the kernel of Johnson's book of the Journey. Once one has come to terms with casually used words like *operose* (laborious) and *perflation* (blowing through), which are themselves part of the joyous texture of his writing, one can revel in the depth of his thought and philosophy. It is the chapter which bears most re-reading and gives a fascinating picture of Highland life of the time. It must be remembered of course that it was written in the comfort of London after he had had time to distill and digest his experiences; this is the philosophical Johnson interpreting the interactions of history, language, religion and environment on the moulding of a race.

'father of Ossian' (p. 140) is Johnson's scornful description of James Macpherson, and the phrase manages to imply that the works were bastard which, of course, they were; and the tragedy is that elementary honesty on Macpherson's part would have given his writings a validity of their own. Macpherson was later to threaten Johnson with physical violence for the comments made in the

chapter *Ostig*. One of the more interesting moments of the great resurrection will be when they come face to face, as they might well do since they are both buried in Westminster Abbey.

'*Col*' (**p. 142ff**) – the island of Coll as we know it now. It was certainly not on Johnson's original itinerary. By sheer chance he met the young Laird of Coll in Talisker in Skye and they became firm friends. With a little persuasion Johnson agreed to break his journey to Iona in order to call on young Maclean of Coll's superior, Sir Allan Maclean, on the island of Inchkenneth. But fate took a hand in things and, having survived a violent 'tempest' on the way from Skye Johnson found himself stranded on Coll for more than a week; he was grateful to be anywhere after the kind of voyage which he'd endured and since he regarded 'being in a ship as being in a gaol, with the chance of being drowned'. Today one can get to Coll in relative comfort by passenger boat from Oban. It is one of the most beautiful islands in the Hebrides but it could be explored very fully in the time Johnson was there, being only twelve miles long by three miles wide. Most of the island is owned now by a millionaire Dutchman, Dr Jan de Vries, but that is a situation which can change at any moment. Buying and selling chunks of the Scottish Highlands is a popular pastime for wealthy Dutchmen.

'*fencible*' (**p. 147**) is one of the more interesting Scottish words that slipped into Johnson's vocabulary too late to be incorporated in his own dictionary. It means *capable of defending* or *fit for active service*. Various Scottish regiments were known by their territorial allegiances, e.g. The Argyllshire Fencibles.

Tobermory (**p. 155**) was an attractive little village even in Dr Johnson's day, but eighty years later it was rebuilt as a model village by the British Fisheries Board in 1888 when the National conscience rebelled against the genocidal policy which had operated against the Highlands since Culloden. Tobermory is one of the great yachting paradises of Great Britain; its bay is famous for the allegedly gold-laden Spanish galleon that sank there in 1588. It is the property (by Royal Charter) of the Dukes of Argyll who make sporadic attempts to raise it, and will probably try again – inspired, perhaps, by the success of the *Mary Rose* operation!

'*Ulva*' (**p. 159–160**). Johnson didn't see very much of the island of Ulva, not so much because of his eyesight this time but because he arrived in the dark of a winter's evening and left in the morning. The island was the home of the small but effective Clan MacQuarrie for 800 years. There were several hundred people on Ulva in Johnson's day; now the population is just over 20. It was in Ulva that Johnson heard of 'mercheta mulierum' (p. 160) which he defines as *a tax payable to the Laird on the marriage of a virgin*. Nobody likes to enquire why the custom is now discontinued.

'Inch Kenneth' (p. 160). As he did with 'Ostig' Johnson uses 'Inch Kenneth' as a 'blanket' chapter heading covering the whole of the rest of his journey, and as in 'Ostig' we see the depth of his thought and the subtlety of his assessments. Inchkenneth was his staging post for Iona, but the island was not much behind Iona in its religious connotations; its atmosphere moved Johnson so much that he composed the Latin verses *Insula Sancti Kennethi* and Boswell was to confess rather coyly later that he felt constrained to slip away from the company during the evening and kneel before one of the old Celtic crosses and pray.

'Iona' (p. 166ff) – *alias* 'Icolmkill'. Johnson himself summed up the glory of Iona more eloquently than anybody else has ever done. It is a place to be experienced rather than seen; to be felt rather than visited. Miraculously Iona survives an inrush of half a million tourists every summer and it is not too fanciful to say that the reason is that the person who goes to the island as a tourist steps ashore as a pilgrim.

Once he left Iona, Dr Johnson's interest in the rest of the tour was, obviously, wilting slightly, and he wrapped up the rest of his narrative in an economy of words that wasn't entirely characteristic. He did note

Duart Castle (p. 179) as he sailed up the Sound of Mull. It was deserted then and had been for more than a century since the Macleans were crushed by the Campbells. It was recovered and restored by Sir Fitzroy Maclean in 1936, and it is now the home of the present Chief of Clan Maclean who happens also to be the Lord Chamberlain who organizes functions celebrating Royal births, marriages and deaths, and enthronements.

Oban (p. 186ff) saw Johnson back on the mainland again, and he does scant credit to the beauty of the scenery that he passed through on his way to Inveraray, Loch Lomond and Auchinleck on his way to Edinburgh and the post-chaise for London.

Epilogue

NOBODY WILL EVER KNOW why Dr Johnson chose to visit the Highlands in Autumn and early Winter, any more than anyone will ever know how some of his judgements might have been tempered had he accompanied Boswell when the latter came north in the late Spring. The summer of 1773 had been an exceptionally fine one in the Highlands; so much so that when the two travellers visited the famous Falls of Foyers on 30 August they found them reduced to a mere trickle after the prolonged drought! After that the heavens opened, and in the whole of September they had only one and a half dry days and about the same in October. Three dry days out of sixty-one would be enough to depress the most enthusiastic fresh air fiend with to-day's comforts of travel and accommodation to fall back on; it was a miracle that a wheezy, over-weight 64-year-old, sleeping rough for a lot of the time, survived at all. Of course a summer visit wouldn't have suited Boswell who was tied up with the Edinburgh law courts till August; he would have missed what he himself described (having got Johnson as far as Skye) as the delight of 'a dog who has got hold of a large piece of meat, and runs away with it to a corner, where he may devour it in peace, without fear of others taking it from him'. The analogy was not one of Boswell's happier ones; the dog with the piece of meat would have missed out on the joy of showing off his capture.

A Journey to the Western Islands has a vague reputation of being an anti-Scottish and anti-Highland book. It is not in fact. Johnson went on record as saying that the time spent in the tour was the pleasantest part of his life. While he was staying at Boswell's parental home in Auchinleck he was asked how he liked the Highlands and his reply was 'How, Sir, can you ask me what obliges me to speak unfavourably of a country where I have been hospitably entertained? Who *can* like the Highlands? I like the inhabitants very well.' Had Dr Johnson seen the Highlands with the eyesight and under the same conditions enjoyed by Mr Jon Wyand (who covered the same ground at the same time of the year to take the photographs for this book) then the tone of the *Journey* might have been rather different.

When reading Johnson's account, it is important to remember what conditions were like in the north of Scotland at the end of the eighteenth century. In 1773, the battle of Culloden was only 27 years away; the country was still garrisoned; the Act banning the wearing of the Highland dress was still in force; The Clan system was being dismantled, and not only was the power of the Chiefs being eroded but they themselves were being seduced towards an alien culture. (Sir Alexander Macdonald, the Chief of Clan Donald who entertained Johnson and Boswell at Armadale, was educated at Eton and probably had more in common with Boswell and his society than he had with the vast majority of his own clansfolk.) Emigration, which was to reach horrific proportions in the nineteenth century, was beginning to be chosen as a preferable alternative to life in the Highlands by such people as had the imagination and the means to seek that course, and the tragedy for the Highlands at that stage was that they were largely the natural leaders of the community and the most enterprising people who were beginning to seek new lives on the other side of the Atlantic.

The subject of emigration had been discussed during Johnson's brief stay in Edinburgh at the start of the journey and he had condemned it as hurtful to human happiness, 'For it spreads mankind, which weakens the defence of a nation, and lessens the comfort of living. Men, thinly scattered, make a shift, but a bad shift, without many things. A smith is ten miles off; they'll do without a nail or a staple. A tailor is far from them; they'll botch their own clothes. It is being concentrated which produces high convenience.' The argument was slightly tangential to the Highland situation with which Johnson had not come in direct contact, but elements of it were applicable nevertheless. For a brief while emigration from the Highlands was to be prohibited because Highlanders suddenly came into demand as fighting men for the Napoleonic Wars, and as collectors of kelp.

When Johnson reached the West Highlands, however, despite being cushioned from the generality of the population by the language barrier and the social standing of those who hosted him, he was too shrewd not to grasp some of the realities of the situation. In the long dissertation written in London but lumped into his longest chapter *Ostig in Sky* he says

That causes very different from want of room may produce a general disposition to seek another country, is apparent from the present conduct of the Highlanders, who are in some places ready to threaten a total secession. The numbers which have already gone, though like other numbers they may be magnified, are very great, and such as, if they had gone together and agreed upon any certain settlement, might have founded an independent government in the depths of the western continent. Nor are they only the lowest and most indigent; many men of considerable wealth have taken with them their train of labourers and dependants; and if they continue the feudal scheme of polity, may establish new Clans in the other hemisphere.

That the immediate motives of their desertion must be imputed to their landlords may be reasonably concluded, because some lairds of more prudence and less rapacity have kept their vassals undiminished. From Raasay only one man had been seduced, and at Col there was no wish to go away.'

In that *dissertation* as I've called it, Johnson is making three separate points. He is forecasting, with extraordinary accuracy, what did happen in the nineteenth century when emigration and ruthless eviction combined to drive tens of thousands of Highlanders to Canada where they congregated in their distinctive communities and where their descendants survive to this day as vital Gaelic speaking communities in Nova Scotia and Cape Breton Island. He is paying a handsome compliment to MacLeod of Raasay and to Maclean of Coll who had been generous hosts to him and who up to that time had not embarked on a policy of land clearance in favour of sheepfarming. The veiled charge of 'rapacity' is levelled in particular at Sir Alexander Macdonald who was just beginning to exploit the newly developing kelp industry. Kelp

was the large brown seaweed which proliferated on the northwest coast of Scotland. When it was burnt its ash provided valuable ingredients for the making of soda and glass and iodine and from the 1760s onwards its commercial value soared and Clan chiefs turned landlords made vast profits by slave labouring their tenants whom they herded into coastal labour camps and employed under conditions compared with which the state of the American negro slaves was reckoned to be paradise. The industry was just being developed when Johnson was in the Highlands; his host at Armadale, who was to become the first Lord Macdonald, was soon to be coining an income of £20,000 a year from the trade. It was, in fact, on a kelp boat that Johnson and Boswell left Skye on their hazardous journey to Coll.

The chapter *Ostig in Sky* is Johnson at his reflective and philosophical best.

The highlight of his visit was his stay at Dunvegan Castle, despite the fact that the weather was particularly appalling and that he was confined to bed with a heavy cold. At Dunvegan (now the oldest inhabited Clan castle in Scotland) he saw the nearest approach to the traditional Clan Chief's establishment even although Norman, the 23rd Chief of Macleod, had inherited debts to the tune of £40,000 and an assured income of only £1,300 a year. 'If he gets the better of this, he'll be a hero,' said Johnson, 'and I hope he will. I have not met with a young man who had more desire to learn, or who had learnt more. I have seen nobody that I wish more to do a kindness to than MacLeod'.) Young MacLeod of MacLeod who had inherited the title (and the debt) from his grandfather at the age of 19 was an excellent landlord, and although he does not comment on it, Johnson was, in all probability, aware of this. Certainly Boswell was; in his journal of the tour he calls Macleod 'a most promising youth, who with a noble spirit struggles with difficulties, and endeavours to preserve his people'. This awareness of the responsibilities of Chiefship was a characteristic of many of the Chiefs Dunvegan; in 1847, when the great potato famine savaged the Highlands, the grandson of Johnson's host was spending up to £300 a week feeding between six and seven thousand of his people, and, in the end, had to lease Dunvegan Castle and take a job as a junior clerk in London.

The 23rd MacLeod of MacLeod had been a student of a friend of Johnson's at University

College, Oxford, and he went out of his way to bring a host of leading Skyemen to meet Johnson. Instead of treating the old man with awe, M.cLeod treated him with great good humour, and noticing how intrigued Johnson was to discover that many Highland lairds were named after their territories (MacLeod of Raasay was Raasay; Maclean of Coll was known as Coll) he offered Johnson the island of Isay at the mouth of Loch Dunvegan on condition that he came to live there for at least one month every year and that he be known as *Island Isay*. The idea tickled Johnson's fancy and he wrote to Mrs Thrale saying 'Macleod has offered me an island; if it were not too far off I should hardly refuse it; my island would be pleasanter than Brighthelmstone if you and my master could come to it; but I cannot think it pleasant to live quite alone.' Alas Johnson never even saw Isay; the weather was too foul for the whole of his stay.

He slept in the Fairy Room of Dunvegan Castle, and revelled in the idea. Unfortunately, the Fairy Flag (which is supposed to save the Clan MacLeod from disaster on three occasions and is alleged to have done so twice) was locked away in an iron chest and nobody thought of mentioning its existence to him. It now hangs on the wall of the castle in a glass case, with one 'life' to go, and near it hangs the letter which Johnson wrote to thank MacLeod and his mother for their kindness. The Dowager Lady MacLeod (the *Lady* was a courtesy title) treated her guest with rather more firmness than her son. She thought he was the ugliest thing she had seen in her life when she went upstairs to visit him in his sickbed and found him sitting up in bed grumpily with his wig on inside out against the cold. Theirs was a sparring relationship. Having served him with his sixteenth cup of tea (not an unusual number for him) she asked if a small basin wouldn't perhaps save him trouble and be more agreeable. 'I wonder, Madam,' he growled, 'why all the ladies ask me such impertinent questions. It is to save yourselves trouble, Madam, and not me.' She had already rubbed him on the raw by coaxing him to have a brandy for the sake of his cold and he had been forced into admitting that he couldn't take drink in moderation. 'I am sure sir you would not carry it too far' she had said. 'Nay, madam, it carried me' he retorted, and admitted that he had taken advantage of a long illness to give up drink completely. (On only one other occasion was he tempted to take alcohol during the course of the

journey; his curiosity made him drink a gill of whisky in the inn at Inveraray, on their way back south, 'to know what it is that makes a Scotsman happy'. He thought it preferable to any English malt brandy!)

If Johnson 'tasted lotus' at Dunvegan and revelled in the company of young MacLeod, he still had to meet his favourite character of the journey. After leaving Dunvegan they went to Talisker where one of their fellow guests was Donald Maclean, the heir of the Laird of Coll. Maclean had spent some time studying farming in Hertfordshire and Hampshire, and his advanced outlook and his intelligence immediately appealed to Johnson. Which was just as well because they were destined to spend eleven days together when bad weather stranded Boswell and Johnson on the little island of Coll. Unlike Maclean, many of the people from whom Johnson gleaned his information had been, one way or another, educated away from their roots and so, unable to communicate with ordinary Highlanders because of the language barrier; so it was inevitable that many of the prejudices that he came away with were just confirmations of his original ones. The miracle was that he came away with so much sympathy with the people despite the fact that he failed to grasp that 'mountaineers' could be custodians of a culture even if not a great deal of it was in print. 'In an unwritten speech', he says 'nothing that is not very short is transmitted from one generation to another. Few have opportunities of hearing a long composition often enough to learn it, or have an inclination to repeat it so often as is necessary to retain it.' It was this kind of assertion which laid him open to attack in some quarters when *A Journey to the Western Islands* was published. Nobody had told him, obviously, that there were at least three poets — major by any European standards — composing poetry of superb standard and epic length at the very time that he was travelling the Highlands. Duncan Ban MacIntyre, Rob Donn MacKay, and Alexander Macdonald. The first two of those couldn't write, but thousands of lines of their poetry survived. Not only could Alexander Macdonald write but he had his published poems burnt at the Mercat Cross in Edinburgh after the Forty-Five, and, like Johnson himself, was a lexicographer of his own native language.

Johnson's *Journey* got what is nowadays called a mixed reception in Scotland. Thomas Knox who did a tour of Scotland similar to Johnson's own wrote

I have read his book again and again, travelled with him from Berwick to Glenelg, through countries with which I am well acquainted; sailed with him from Glenelg to Raasay, Sky, Rum, Coll, Mull and Icolmkill; but have not been able to correct him in any matter of consequence. I have often admired the accuracy, the precision, and the justness of what he advances respecting both the country and the people.

The Doctor has everywhere delivered his sentiments with freedom, and in many instances with a seeming regard for the benefit of the inhabitants and the ornament of the country. His remarks on the want of trees and hedges for shade, as well as for shelter to the cattle, are well founded, and merit the thanks, not the illiberal censure of the natives. He also felt for the distresses of the Highlanders and explodes with great propriety the bad management of the grounds, and the neglect of timber in the Hebrides.

Professor Alexander Tytler of Edinburgh University wrote

I read Dr Johnson's Tour with very great pleasure. Some few errors he has fallen into, but of no great importance, and those are lost in the numberless beauties of his work. If I had leisure I could perhaps point out the most exceptional places; but at present I am in the country and have not his book at hand. It is plain he meant to speak well of Scotland; and he has, in my apprehension, done us great honour. . . .

The Scots Magazine and *The Edinburgh Monthly Review* both carried extensive extracts from the *Journey* but carefully left their readers to arrive at their own conclusions.

Needless to say James Macpherson, author of the 'Ossianic translations' denounced a dozen years earlier as fakes, didn't find the book either edifying or amusing but, unfortunately, his letter to Dr Johnson does not survive. One can guess at its contents, however, from Johnson's reply and the conclusion is that he threatened to break the great man's neck or worse.

Mr James Macpherson — I received your foolish and impudent letter. Any violence offered me I shall do my best to repel; and

what I cannot do for myself the law shall do for me. I hope I shall never be deterred from detecting what I think a cheat, by the menaces of a ruffian.

What would you have me retract? I thought your book an imposture; I think it is an imposture still. For this opinion I have given my reasons to the public, which I here dare you to refute. Your rage I defy. Your abilities, since your Homer, are not so formidable; and what I hear of your morals inclines me to pay regard not to what you shall say, but to what you shall prove. You may print this if you will.

Sam. Johnson

Far and away the most vituperative attack on *A Journey to the Western Islands* came in 1779 (four years after the publication of Johnson's book) when the Revd Donald MacNicol, minister of the island of Lismore in Argyll published a book approximately the same length as Johnson's own tearing the *Journey* apart almost paragraph by paragraph. MacNicol was, himself, a collector of Gaelic poetry and folk legends and was, in many ways, well qualified to attack Johnson's generalizations on Gaelic literature. His over-enthusiasm was self defeating. Many of his criticisms were carping, and although he could demolish the means by which Johnson had arrived at his conclusion that James Macpherson's works were fake, he could not deny the fact that Johnson's conclusion was, nevertheless, correct.

MacNicol's preface to his own book makes rather ironical reading now:

The following sheets were written soon after *Dr Johnson's Journey to the Hebrides* [he even got the title wrong] was printed. But as the writer had never made his appearance at the bar of the Public, he was unwilling to enter the lists, with such a *powerful* antagonist, without previously consulting a few learned friends. The distance of those friends made it difficult to procure their opinion, without some trouble and a great loss of time: besides, the Author was not so fond of his work as to be very anxious about its publication.

He is, however, sensible, that the publication, if it was at all to happen, has been too long delayed. Answers to eminent writers are generally indebted, for their sale and circulation, to the works which they endeavour to refute. Unfortunately, Dr Johnson's *Journey* has lain dead in the library for some time past. This consideration is so discouraging, that the writer of the Remarks expects little literary reputation, and less profit, from his labours. But, as he had gone so far, he was induced to go further still, were it for nothing more than the ambition of sending his work to *sleep*, on the same shelf, with that of the learned Dr Johnson.

Poor MacNicol. His intentions were honourable. But he chose a restless bedfellow for his *Remarks*. Johnson's *Journey* has been revised, editionized and regurgitated in so many forms that it would be difficult and futile to count them. MacNicol might have fared better had he adopted some of the modesty (untypical though it might be) of Johnson himself when he ended his book with the words 'Novelty and ignorance must always be reciprocal, and I cannot but be conscious that my thoughts on national matters, are the thoughts of one who has seen but little.'

How times and attitudes change is demonstrated beautifully in a speech given by the distinguished Highland historian W. C. MacKenzie to the Gaelic Society of Inverness in 1927 when the Highlands were still enmeshed in their own romance and much more sensitive to criticism than they are now. MacKenzie's subject was *Dr Johnson and the Western Isles* and he summed up his carefully constructed speech as follows:

What, it may be asked, was the outstanding feature of the relations between the illustrious guest and his Highland hosts? It may, I think, be described as mutual liking, founded upon mutual esteem.

Johnson was seen in the Hebrides in a variety of moods. He was genial and peevish by turns. But his geniality was inspired by the people while his peevishness was generally caused by the weather. Sometimes a patient listener — he *listened* sometimes — he was occasionally an irritable down-shouter. Yet his sympathy could always be enlisted by sincerity, though his anger was always aroused by fatuities. He was congenitally incapacitated from suffering

fools gladly. But he doesn't seem to have met many of them in the Isles. As a philosopher he should have been immune, no doubt, from giving way to petty vexations. But he was very human. He set up standards for other people which he was quite willing to admit were impossible of attainment for himself.

As to the other side of the picture, is it not a surprising reflection that this scrofulous old man, undistinguished physically except for his bulk, without rank, without wealth, without ancestry, without any of the ouward accessories that impress a people peculiarly susceptible to these influences, should have been received in the Highlands as if he were a prince of Scottish blood, instead of a mere English publicist {sic} of plebeian birth?

Johnson's Jacobitism does not explain the anomaly, though it explains, perhaps, in part, his reciprocal regard for the Highland people. Does it not connote a degree of culture in the Highlands a century and a half ago with which the Highlands are seldom credited? For consider, it was the wit and the wisdom, the scholarship and the intellectual strength of Johnson that set him on a pinnacle in Fleet Street from which he was made visible in the remote Hebrides. The name of Johnson was revered by the obscure student in the Isles no less than by the man of letters in Edinburgh. His reputation as a great man and a good man was nowhere higher than in the lonely manses of the Highlands and the lordly castles of the Hebrides. And the common people, with a vague sense of his distinction, were no less ready to do him reverence. From the ragged loon who tried to amuse him by saying 'See such pretty goats' and by making the goats jump for his diversion, right up in the social scale to MacCailein Mor himself, who entertained him at Inveraray Castle, and sat at his feet for instruction, all classes sought to honour their celebrated visitor. And I conclude by expressing my conviction that, considered either from the personal standpoint or from that of international amenities, Johnson's tour was a landmark in the history of the

Hebrides which we would not willingly obliterate.

There still remains the question why Johnson in his sixty-fourth year (he celebrated his sixty-fourth birthday in Dunvegan) should ever have set out on a journey which would have dismayed a fit young man in the conditions of 1773. I have quoted the three most obvious possible explanations – the curiosity that Martin Martin implanted in his youthful mind, the wish to destroy the reputation of James Macpherson, and the importuning of James Boswell. In his unpretentious and excellent book *Samuel Johnson*, John Wain advances a more subtle argument.

All his life he [Johnson] had longed for some means of comparing the present system with that of earlier days. Did money, social flexibility, ease of communication, really produce happiness, or was the old, fixed, earth-rooted pyramid better? What was life *really* like in historical times? He was a passionate student of history; but the professional historians, prosing on about battles and treaties and alliances, had never satisfied him. As he was later to remark to Boswell (29 April 1778) 'All that is really *known* of the ancient state of Britain is contained in a few pages. . . . I would wish to have one branch well done, and that is the history of manners, of common life.' And there, all the time, within his own nation-state, governed (nominally) by the same king and parliament that governed him, was a feudal society that had lived on into his own day; a society which rarely handled money, where the laird received his rent in goods and services and had jurisdiction over his people. To travel only a few hundred miles north would have been to see this society, to mingle with it, and to gain a more vivid impression of what mediaeval feudalism must have been like than could have been gathered from all the historians that ever wrote.

But the Vanity of Human Wishes was manifested here as it was everywhere else. This state of affairs lasted only until 1745. And though Johnson might well have wished to travel to the Hebrides before that date, might have wished it as he pored over Martin Martin's *Description of the Western Islands of Scotland* in his father's shop, he might as realistically have wished to go to the moon. Now he was free and able to make the journey; he had made it; and the feudal society, in anything like its pure state was thirty years back in the past. . . . What he found was not a feudal society. But it was something equally interesting, and equally challenging to his powers of description and analysis: a society in the agonies of change.

Whatever reason sent him he returned to London on 26 November fit and apparently unwearied by his days on the road. On 27 November he wrote to Boswell, who had remained in Edinburgh

Dear Sir – I came home last night without any incommodity, danger, or weariness, and am ready to begin a new journey . . .

'He [Dr Johnson] said to me often that the time he spent in this tour was the pleasantest part of his life, and asked me if I would lose recollection of it for five hundred pounds. I answered I would not, and he applauded my setting such a value on an accession of new images in my mind. Had it not been for me, I am persuaded Dr Johnson never would have undertaken such a journey; and I must be allowed some merit for having been the cause that our language has been enriched with such a book as that which he published on his return.'
Jas. Boswell

Johnson's journey with approximate mileages for his route – not always direct and often by sea (ferry distances very suppositious)

1773

Saturday 14 August	Johnson arrives in Edinburgh
Wednesday 18 August	Boswell and Johnson cross Firth of Forth to Kinghorn, then 30 miles to St Andrews
Friday 20 August	to Montrose (43 miles)
Saturday 21 August	to Aberdeen (38 miles)
Tuesday 24 August	via Ellon to Slains (25 miles)
Wednesday 25 August	to Banff (45 miles)
Thursday 26 August	to Forres (47 miles)
Friday 27 August	to Cawdor (16 miles)
Saturday 28 August	via Fort George to Inverness (17 miles)
Monday 30 August	to Fort Augustus (32 miles)
Tuesday 31 August	Fort Augustus (overnight at Anoch)
Wednesday 1 September	to Glenelg (50 miles from Fort Augustus)
Thursday 2 September	by sea 15 miles to Armadale in Skye
Monday 6 September	touring on Skye
Tuesday 7 September	continue tour of Skye, then by sea 10 miles to Raasay
Sunday 12 September	by sea 5 miles to Portree, then 12 miles to Kingsburgh
Monday 13 September	by sea 5 miles to south of Loch Greshornish, then 7 miles to Dunvegan
Friday 17 September	excursion to Annait
Tuesday 21 September	Dunvegan to Ullinish
Wednesday 22 September	excursion to Broch
Thursday 23 September	by sea 7 miles to Fernilea, then 3 miles to Talisker
Saturday 25 September	Talisker to Coirechatachan
Tuesday 28 September	to Ostaig (45 miles from Talisker)
Friday 1 October	to Armadale (2 miles)
Sunday 3 October	by sea 35 miles to anchorage off Coll
Monday 4 October	land on Coll
Thursday 14 October	by sea 20 miles to Tobermory, then 10 miles to Erray
Saturday 16 October	short sea crossing to Ulva
Sunday 17 October	short sea passage to Inchkenneth
Tuesday 19 October	by sea 10 miles to Mackinnon's Cave on Mull, then Iona
Wednesday 20 October	by sea 20 miles to Ardcrishnish
Thursday 21 October	to Lochbuie (20 miles)
Friday 22 October	by sea 20 miles to Oban
Saturday 23 October	to Inveraray (25 miles)
Tuesday 26 October	Inveraray to Rossdhu (35 miles)
Wednesday 27 October	on Loch Lomond 10 miles to Cameron
Thursday 28 October	to Glasgow (19 miles)

From Glasgow Johnson went on to visit Boswell's father at Auchinleck before returning to Edinburgh. He left Scotland on 22 November.